THE
CHRISTIAN YEAR

THE

CHRISTIAN

YEAR

by EDWARD T. *raill* HORN, III

MUHLENBERG PRESS • PHILADELPHIA

FOREWORD

In writing about the Christian year, it is almost impossible to know where to begin, or where to stop. The editing of the *Acta Sanctorum,* accounts of the saints assigned to each day, was begun by a group of ecclesiastical scholars, known as the Bollandists, in the seventeenth century. The accounts already comprise scores of folio volumes and remain incomplete. Variations among ancient calendars and martyrologies still attract the attention of liturgical scholars.

What most Christians want to know, however, is how the present church year came to be; why certain dates are as they are, without much seeming logic or reason; and certain very practical matters such as the sources of the variable lessons and chants, and the proper altar colors. These latter are the means by which the Western church adjusts the invariable framework of its worship to the particular occasion.

Some of the historical data are admittedly quite hazy. When that is so, general terms have been employed. The "apostolic church" refers to the church in the first generation of Christians; "primitive church" refers to the period from the end of the apostolic age to the Edict of Toleration in 313, when Christianity became a legal religion and could for the first time operate publicly without fear of persecution.

I am indebted to many people, but especially to my colleagues on the Joint Commission on the Common Liturgy, and to those who served with me on the former Common Service Book Committee of The United Lutheran Church in America, for making me investigate the Christian Year and thus discover much that appears in the following pages.

Trinity Church,   EDWARD TRAILL HORN, III
Germantown, Philadelphia,
Ash Wednesday, 1956.

TABLE OF CONTENTS

INTRODUCTION

There has been a revival of interest in liturgical matters in all branches of the Christian church in recent years. In churches which were conservative at the time of the Reformation, this has meant the deepening of appreciation of the common heritage of the Western church. In churches which were more radical in the sixteenth century, it has meant the recovery of long lost traditions and observances. Among these is the Christian year. Lutherans and Anglicans have enriched their calendars; the Church of Scotland has recovered much that once belonged to it.

The Lutheran reader of these pages will be somewhat acquainted with much of the background. In America, a new *Service Book* is to be used by six million Lutherans in English-speaking countries. Unlike either Roman or Anglican service books, it includes both the liturgy and the hymnal in one bound volume. It is one of the most important Lutheran orders ever produced.

The first permanent Lutheran settlers founded Fort Caroline on the southern coast of the United States in 1562. Two years later they were wiped out by the Spaniard, Menendez, who came north from Florida and put them all to the sword "not as Frenchmen, but as Lutherans." Lutherans formed the ill-fated expedition of Danes on the shore of Hudson Bay in 1619, and were among the earliest settlers of New Amsterdam in 1623. In 1638, the Swedes settled at Fort Christina on the Delaware River and brought their state church with them. Later, but long before the American Revolution, Lutherans

1

poured into New York and especially Pennsylvania, where today there are still more Lutherans than in any other state. From Pennsylvania they traveled down the Shenandoah Valley of Virginia into the Piedmont of North and South Carolina. They exerted strong influence on other denominations. Lutheran Salzburgers, emigrating to America on the same ship as the Wesleys, made a profound impression on the founders of Methodism by their piety, faith and hymnody. William Augustus Muhlenberg, one of the most distinguished clergymen and liturgiologists of the Protestant Episcopal church, was a grandson of Henry Melchior Muhlenberg, patriarch and organizer of the American Lutheran church in the middle eighteenth century.

After the Revolution there was a temporary slackening of Lutheran immigration, especially from European countries then without any hope of establishing permanent overseas empires. But by the middle of the nineteenth century immigration from Lutheran countries had reached a new peak and maintained a constant flow until about 1910.

In most of the areas of Europe in which it was established, the Lutheran church was the state church—in all of Scandinavia and in much of what is now Germany. It had the official support of the government; it was financed by taxes; its clergy were civil as well as religious officebearers. People were "born" into the Lutheran church and remained in its membership unless they declared themselves out of it. For Lutheran immigrants the American free church system, under which no one belonged to any church unless he actively sought membership, was quite strange. The result was that many members of the first generation in America did not join their church here at all, and that many second and third generation descendants joined other churches due to the weakening of their Lutheran ties.

No other church faced the same difficulties in transition from foreign tongues to English. The only church which sent to America immigrants from as many different countries as the Lutheran church was the Roman Catholic church. But the Roman Catholic church used Latin universally in its mass, while in the Lutheran church the service was in the vernacular, the language of the people. Lutherans from Germany, Sweden, Norway, Denmark, Finland, Slovakia, Iceland, France, Hungary, Esthonia, Latvia, Lithuania and other lands brought the Lutheran liturgy to America in their native tongues. In many cases they were quite loath to surrender to English, for the religious use of their native language was an anchor binding them to their homelands and to the cultures they had left there. The result was that their children, born in America, often left the "foreign" churches of their parents. If there were English-language Lutheran churches at hand, they often joined them. But, with the tide of foreign immigration so high and with such a large proportion of foreign-trained clergymen necessary, the synods of the church were less progressive than they should have been in the establishment of English Lutheran churches.

American Lutheranism has had to produce its own leadership and its own liturgy. European Lutheran theologians still tend to regard American Lutheranism in a rather condescending manner, though there is a growing awareness that the church of the Augsburg Confession has not been "de-Lutheranized" just because it has become Anglicized in America. Contemporary American Protestantism, the other possible source of help, has not contributed much. For a time, before the founding of a seminary in 1828, native Lutheran ministers were trained privately or in seminaries of other churches. The result was a watered-down Lutheranism which flirted with "new measures," until it was overwhelmed by new Lutheran immigration. The only sister church with a similar tradition and liturgy was the Protestant Episcopal church, but it either ignored the Lutheran church as an immigrant group, or attempted to make Episcopalians out of second and third generation Lutherans, especially the Swedes. The old, historic Swedish churches along the Delaware River, founded before 1700, had all passed into Episcopal hands by one means or another before 1850.

In the area of the liturgy, the problem was complicated even more by the fact that the prevailing American temper was non- and often antiliturgical. This despite the fact that lodges and secret societies with elaborate rituals and uniforms flourished in every small village only one generation removed from the wilderness. When it came to religion, however, early America appeared to prefer the camp meeting type. The cultural climate was not sympathetic to the liturgical church. This affected the Lutheran church more than either the Protestant Episcopal or Roman Catholic churches, since the efforts of the latter two were confined largely to the cities, while the Lutheran churches from Pennsylvania to Georgia were largely in the open country or small towns.

Nevertheless, one of the important objectives achieved by Muhlenberg was the first American Lutheran liturgy in 1786. It was in German. Not until 1860 did the first official Lutheran liturgy appear in English. The standard English language Lutheran liturgy appeared in 1888 as the *Common Service,* and it has become the accepted Lutheran liturgy in America. The new *Service Book* is based on the *Common Service* of 1888, but, while the latter was based exclusively on the German church orders of the sixteenth century, the former includes the Scandinavian orders of Reformation provenance as well as adjustments to the needs of the present day.

In setting the liturgy into English, Lutheran scholars discovered that much of their work had been done for them.

Henry Eyster Jacobs in his book *The Lutheran Movement in England* established two facts: first, that the Sarum and other English missals upon which the Anglican liturgy is based, were in agreement with the Bamberg, Mainz, Constance, Augsburg and other German missals upon which the Lutheran orders were based; and second, that the two years which Archbishop Cranmer spent in Germany profoundly influenced the First Prayer Book of Edward VI, which made its appearance shortly after Cranmer's return to England. This influence has never been completely measured. Cranmer married the niece of Osiander, pastor in Nuremberg and one of the liturgical leaders of the Lutheran Reformation. Through him, Cranmer became acquainted with the liturgical reforms being prepared for Cologne by Archbishop Herman von Wied, and which appeared in 1543. It is not surprising then, that both Lutheran and Anglican orders are similar, and in many respects identical.

Anglican scholars have been loath to concede much Lutheran influence on the English Prayer Book. Lutherans, however, freely acknowledge their debt to the English book. Many of the collects for the church year, occasional services, and orders had been put into such fine classic English in the Prayer Book that, in most cases, any new attempts at translation would have been wasted effort. Some of the items had, by the nineteenth century, become English classics in their own right, and the Lutheran church adopted them for its English language use.

On the other hand, the Lutheran church could not accept the Great Bible version of the psalter. Instead it accepted, with the rest of the English-speaking world, the King James version of the Bible for its lessons and psalms. It was also thrown on its own resources for English versions of the introits and graduals, since the *Book of Common Prayer* does not include the historic series of either chant. Here the problem was a difficult one because the version used in the pre-Reformation

missals was the text of the ancient Itala version—the oldest
Latin translation, which was in use before the Vulgate. Rather
than make all the chants conform to the King James version's
text, the Lutheran church uses an English translation of the
Latin Itala for the introits and graduals. This explains the
slight differences in psalm verses from the well-known and
accepted text.

In general, it may be claimed that the Lutheran use is closer
to the historic use of Western Christianity than is that of any
other church. In some respects, it is more Roman than the
church of Rome itself, as for instance in the continuing Lutheran custom (discarded by the Roman Catholic church) of
naming the Sundays in Lent and after Easter by the opening
words of their ancient Latin introits. And some of the usages
of the ancient Gallican rite from which some of the German
missals antecedent to Lutheran use developed, antedate the
Roman rite which replaced them in 1570.

The Lutheran liturgy and the First Prayer Book of Edward
VI of 1549 were strikingly similar. Were the latter still in use
in Anglican churches, there would be surprising agreement
between the two liturgical non-Roman churches of Western
Christianity. But a strong Calvinistic influence is evident in
the Second Prayer Book of Edward VI in 1552, and subsequent
effort to appease the nonliturgical dissenters widened the gap
in the liturgical practice of the two churches. The main service on Sunday in most Anglican churches is morning prayer,
which is a version of what Lutherans know as matins. Many
regular attendants at Anglican worship hear the historic propers
only on the first Sunday in the month at communion, and on
some festivals. In Lutheran use, the antecommunion is the
normal Sunday service, though the ideal postulated by Luther
and the sixteenth-century church orders was a service with a
sermon and communion every Sunday. The church is slowly

returning to that ideal, but in the meantime the regular at-
tendant at Lutheran worship hears the historic propers—
introit, collect, epistle, gradual, gospel—every Sunday and on
all festivals. By their continued use, the Lutheran church bears
witness to the fact that it is not a new church founded in 1517,
but part of the "one holy catholic and apostolic church"; as
well as to the belief that "it is pleasing to us that, for the sake
of unity and good order, universal rites be observed" (Apology
of the Augsburg Confession, IV, 33); and finally, to its faith
in the continuing presence of the Holy Spirit in the church as
the church comes to God in worship.

1.

GOD AND TIME

The heart of the Christian message is God's revelation of himself, in time, in the person of Jesus Christ, his Son. God's salvation is revealed in the stream of human history. The manger at Bethlehem, the Virgin Mary, the disciples, the cross on Calvary, the empty tomb in the garden, were all "in time," and were transfigured by the eternal presence of God in Christ. Christian faith is rooted in the belief that God has acted in Christ in human history. It was a unique action. Nothing like it, or like the series of remarkable events connected with it, has ever occurred before or since. God chose the time for time and eternity to meet, and time can never be the same again.

The liturgy of the Christian church recognizes this fact and seeks to relate all time to the redemptive purposes of God. The major events of the life of our Lord pass in review perennially in the first half of the church year, keeping the Christian community in perpetual remembrance of "all that our Lord hath done for our sakes." The second half of the church year relates the profound implications of our Lord's incarnation, life, death and resurrection to the life in time of the Christian and of the Christian community.

In addition, special liturgical services mark the successive stages of the life of the Christian in time: baptism, confirmation, marriage, sickness, death. In them the church seeks the blessing of God at moments of decision which are important not only to the individual Christian, but also to the entire community—the church. Such crises have meaning not only in time, but also in eternity. In all of these ways, the church places upon both the ordinary and the extraordinary occasions of life the seal of God. While it is true that God does not reserve the communication of his graces to certain days, it is also true that God does not disdain the use of time as a means of revealing himself. There are occasions on which certain aspects of his presence are more perceptible than ordinarily.

The four weeks of Advent recall the expectation of the coming of the Messiah on the part of the ancient Hebrews on the one hand, and the second coming of the Savior at the end of time on the other. The voices of the prophets and of John the Baptist unite the Christian with an expectant creation whose God is both its beginning and its end. Christmas and Epiphany call the faithful to ponder the mystery of the Incarnation. The Word is made flesh and dwells among us and, for the moment, heaven and earth are one and both ring with joy. On Good Friday, it is not Jesus of Nazareth only who dies on the cross. It is God himself who, in the sacrifice of his Son, reconciles a creation gone astray through the sin of the first Adam. On Easter, the victorious life of Christ passes beyond the bounds of death and betokens an endless life with God for all whose lives are united to him by faith in his Son. On Ascension Day, the Son re-enters the glory of the Godhead. On Pentecost, the descent of the Spirit in tongues of fire and inspiration marks the eruption of the eternal in the world of time.

These recurring events also stimulate corresponding spiritual experiences in the hearts of Christian people. The joy of the Christmas season is a reflection of the birth of the Savior. In Holy Week, it is his death which casts a pall over Christendom. When, at Easter, the church sings its "alleluias" and evidences its optimism and daring faith amid the distress of the world,

it is because Christ is risen and has triumped over death. And
at Pentecost, the feeling of Christian solidarity and of witness-
ing for Christ is due to hearts touched anew by the Holy Spirit.

But the church's year is more than simply an annual cycle
of recurring festivals and fasts. Every day can be an Advent
in which Christ comes anew to our hearts; an Epiphany in
which he is manifested afresh; a Lent in which he suffers for
our sins; an Easter in which he rises again; a Pentecost in which
his Spirit is poured out once more. What happened to God in
time also happens to his people in time. The experiences of
Christ, while unique and totally other because he is God, are
also unique and totally ours because he was also man. His birth
in our hearts at Christmas will make possible our growth into
a measure of his stature. His cross will transfigure human
suffering not only during Lent and Holy Week, but every day.
His Easter triumph overcomes the injustices of daily life and
the fear of death. And otherwise mediocre lives will be lifted
up by the breath of the Spirit, as at Pentecost. In Christ, time
is transfigured, and it becomes possible for us to live each
moment to the greater glory of God.

Ancient religions generally related their worship and its
calendar to natural events: the cycles of the sun or the moon,
the positions of the planets, the procession of seasons, periodic
times of the calving of cattle, of flood and drought, of seedtime
and harvest. The regular recurring rhythm of these natural
events was thought to be evidence of the special presence of
God. In the Graeco-Roman world, for instance, the days of the
week were all named after heavenly bodies: Sun, Moon, Mars,
Mercury, Jupiter, Venus, Saturn. Of these, three—Sunday,
Monday and Saturday—remain in English use.

The ancient Hebrews followed a scheme in which their
festivals were lunar or seasonal. The new moon is bracketed
in importance with the sabbath and appears in some instances

to have been an even greater festival.[1] The Passover was
originally a moon festival in the spring. Its date was determined, as is the date of Easter—its Christian successor—by
the vernal equinox and the full moon.

After the Babylonian captivity, however, the religious
leaders of the Jews began to display a new awareness of the
hand of God in human history. The ancient Hebrew calendar
was reinterpreted and its festivals were associated with the
great historical events of past ages. The Passover then became
significant as the anniversary of the deliverance of the Hebrews
from the bondage of Egypt. It became a commemoration of
an historical event, and had contemporary meaning for all
presently in bondage either to others, or to sin. The Feast of
the Weeks (Pentecost), once a spring festival marking the end
of the barley harvest, became the anniversary of the delivery of
the Law to Moses on Sinai, and a perpetual reminder of the
importance of God's will and of human obedience to it. Since
the events which were commemorated were part of the continuous stream of history, they had meaning not only for their
generation, but also for all who went before and who followed
after. Every devout Hebrew was, therefore, a participant.[2]

The primitive Christian church adopted the later Jewish idea
of the periodic commemoration of historical events in the same
sense, as well as the Jewish festivals of the Passover and Pentecost and the Sabbath. The death of Jesus at the time of the
Passover was quickly interpreted as the sacrifice of the Paschal
Lamb for the deliverance of all men from the bondage of sin.
Possibly, our Lord chose the time and place of his Passion with
this in mind, and the Gospel of John, in particular, draws the

[1] Isa. 1:13 and 66:23, for instance, put the new moons first and the
Sabbaths second. See also Num. 28:11, 16-17; 1 Sam. 20:5; 2 Kings 4:23. Ezek.
46:1, 3; Hos. 2:11; Amos 8:5.
[2] Theodor H. Gaster, *Festivals of the Jewish Year* (New York: William Sloane
Associates, 1953), p. 38.

parallel. The outpouring of the Holy Ghost on the day of Pentecost, when the disciples were "all with one accord in one place" was understood as the day of the founding of the Christian church, superseding the Jewish church founded by the delivery of the Law on Sinai. The Hebrew idea of one day in seven reserved as a day of rest and for the worship of God was continued in the Christian community, though the day became the first day of the week because of the resurrection, rather than the seventh day. In this way, the chief Jewish festivals became the basis of the Christian year. Yet the Hebrew festivals were in no sense carried over, but served only as the type, of which the Christian observance was believed to be the fulfilment.

For the Christian church, moreover, its festivals are more than simply commemorations of past events. They were and are present and living realities. Easter *is* the resurrection of Jesus Christ from the dead with all of its implications, just as truly as it is a commemoration of the dawn in the garden when Mary Magdalene found the empty tomb, and just as truly as it is the foreshadowing of the final hope both of the Christian and of the Christian community. Easter is a revelation in time of which the Christian people are the actual witnesses.

In this way, the Christian church takes the time which God has created and offers it to God through Christ who has redeemed it. The daily and annual cycles of feast and fast constitute the means by which the church, inspired through the ages by the Holy Spirit, does this. It is the church's way of "redeeming the time."

2.

HOW THE CHURCH YEAR
CAME TO BE

It is difficult for twentieth-century Americans to imagine how important the calendar of the church once was in civil life. More than any other country of the modern world except Russia, we are accustomed to an almost completely secular calendar, outside of the fact that we still number our years A.D. (*Anno Domini,* the year of the Lord), and we observe one or two religious festivals, such as Christmas and Good Friday. This is a state of affairs almost unknown in the rest of the world, and not known in parts of America in its earliest days. The annual almanacs published after 1737 in Germantown by Christopher Sauer are studded with the festivals of the church year.

It was, of course, the church which gave the world the present Gregorian calendar, introduced by Pope Gregory XIII in 1582 and given his name, though he did not work it out himself. The "Old Style" or Julian calendar, introduced under Julius Caesar, had an annual error of eleven minutes and four-teen seconds. The "New Style" or Gregorian calendar reduced this error to 26 seconds a year, or one day in 3,323 years. Spain, Portugal, France and Roman Catholic Germany adopted the new calendar at once. Protestant Germany held out until 1700; England until 1752; Sweden until 1753; and Russia until the Bolshevik Revolution of 1918!

During this period there was considerable confusion in western Europe in dating legal documents, births, marriages, and deaths; in travel, trade, and correspondence; and in the church. Because Protestant Germany had adopted the Gregorian calendar in 1700, but England was still using "Old Style" in 1742, Henry Melchior Muhlenberg, setting out for America, celebrated Easter in Hannover on March 25, arrived in London on April 17 (which was April 6 in England), and celebrated Easter again in England on April 18.[1] To further confound matters, the year began on different dates in different places. January 10, 1709, in Scotland was January 10, 1708, in England where the new year began on March 25. In 1751 England and the Colonies adopted January 1 as the beginning of the year. The adjustment to the Gregorian calendar was made in 1752 when the day following September 2 became September 14.

Even though it is more accurate, the Gregorian calendar retains marks of the evolutionary process through which the calendar has developed. February is shorter by from two to three days than any of the other months. There are 181 days in the first half year; 184 in the latter. Holidays with fixed dates, such as February 22 (Washington's Birthday) have a habit of drifting from Sunday to Saturday through the years, resulting in some years in a "long" weekend for working people; in other years, in no holiday at all. There is much to be said in behalf of a fixed calendar in which the days of the month would always fall on the same day of the week, and Easter and the other movable festivals of the church year would cease to move.

Alongside of the Gregorian calendar, there are other calendars in use today. The fiscal year, followed by the government,

[1] T. G. Tappert and J. W. Doberstein (eds.), *The Journals of Henry Melchior Muhlenberg* (Philadelphia: Muhlenberg, 1942), vol. I, pp. 14-19.

banks, and many businesses, runs from July 1 to June 30. The Jewish year begins in September and may have as many as 385 days or as few as 353. School and college years begin in September and end in June. In England, the school terms still bear the names of church festivals near their opening or closing dates such as Michaelmas (September 29) and Trinity (Trinity Sunday, May or June). So the church's year, which begins with the Sunday nearest November 30, continues, though subordinated to the secular calendar.

It was not always so. In medieval times, the secular calendar took second place. The civil holidays were church holidays. Courts recessed, battles ceased, shops were closed, all labor was suspended. With no printed calendars to be hung on his wall, the medieval man depended on the church. As early as the end of the second century in Alexandria, a city famed for astronomy and mathematics, the bishop sent a letter each year to all the churches announcing the date of Easter and the movable festivals dependent upon it. In later centuries, the passage of time was marked by the procession of Sundays and festivals in the church. While this impressed the common man with the importance of the religious life, the multiplication of holydays disrupted agriculture and commerce to such an extent that the reform of the church calendar became almost as pressing as the reform of the church's organization, worship and doctrine. As in these other areas of church life, so the reform of the calendar was a return to an earlier and purer stage in the life of the Christian community.

At its beginning, the church had no church year, just as it had no bishops, no canon law, no New Testament as such, and no creeds. Until the fourth century the church was proscribed in the Roman Empire. While it enjoyed varying degrees of freedom from time to time and from place to place, it always

occupied officially the status of an underground movement. Its
members met in secret. Outside of face-to-face encounters,
Christian communications were often in symbols. Written
letters were often apocalyptic like the Book of Revelation.
Prospective members were examined carefully by a prolonged
series of scrutinies. The church could take no chance of admit-
ting a fifth columnist. It did not dare erect its own buildings.
All of its activities had to be not only unobtrusive, but clan-
destine. The whole political atmosphere was inhospitable to the
development of a church year.

Yet the beginnings of the church year—the distinct manner
in which the church measures time—lie far back of the year
313 when, by the Edict of Toleration, the Emperor Constantine
accorded Christianity legal status in the Roman Empire. The
resurrection of our Lord on Easter Day, the event in which
everything else in the church is rooted, is the source of the
church year. It was the first, and has always been the greatest,
of all festivals and events in the life of the church. Not only
was its annual recurrence marked with high thanksgiving, but,
because our Lord rose from the dead on the first day of the
week, every Sunday became a celebration of the resurrection
and the day of all days when Christians met together.[2] In the
earliest times there seems to have been no separation of the
passion from the resurrection, and the single celebration of the
Pascha at Easter commemorated both.

Second only to Easter, both in date of origin and in early
importance, was Pentecost. It, too, had fallen on a Sunday,
seven weeks after the resurrection. It was while the disciples
were gathered together on the first day of the week in Jerusalem that the Holy Ghost was outpoured upon them and the
Christian church came into being. A few years later, St. Paul

---

[2] Possibly from the very first Sunday after the resurrection. (See John 20:26.)

summoned the Ephesian elders to come to meet him at Miletus because "he hasted . . . to be at Jerusalem the day of Pentecost." [3]

The period bounded by these two festivals, Easter and Pentecost, was the first liturgical season of the church. It was the *Quinquagesima* or Great Fifty Days, and the only season which the church knew during the first three centuries of its existence. As the Hebrews had observed the seven weeks between the Passover and Pentecost as the Omer Days,[4] so the early church maintained throughout the entire fifty days the note of joy and triumph of which Easter was the symbol par excellence. Each of the Sundays was a major festival. There was no fasting during these weeks, and kneeling was forbidden at all services.

The third great early festival, which may go back as far as the end of the first century, was the Epiphany on January 6. It was originally a festival which commemorated the Incarnation—both the birth and the baptism of Christ. Like the Pascha (Easter) and Pentecost, Epiphany took its date from a pre-Christian festival, this time of pagan origin. An ancient festival in Egypt, Arabia, and parts of Palestine celebrated on January 6 the birth of Aeon. This the church replaced with the commemoration of the manifestation of God in Jesus' birth and baptism, since the precise date of both events was not known.

The next items on the Christian calendar were the anniversaries of local martyrs. These were marked by the churches of which they had been members. Almost every congregation in the first four centuries had its own roll of those who had suffered and died for the faith. It was only natural that the dates of their sacrifice should be commemorated in their churches.[5] The calendar of the church in Alexandria would

[3] Acts 20:16.
[4] Lev. 23:15-21.
[5] Today we remember birthdays. The early church remembered its martyrs (John the Baptist excepted) on the date of their birth (*natale*) to life eternal, i.e., their death date.

have its own list. The martyrology of the church in Rome or Carthage would be quite different. Their names were read at the services and commemorative services on their "days" were sometimes held in the cemeteries or catacombs beside their graves. Some of them attained more than local fame (such as Polycarp, Bishop of Smyrna, who was martyred in 156) and their days became fixed in more than one calendar. Others, especially if they happened to belong to less prominent churches, remained parochial martyrs. Some were, with the passage of time and the increasing number of martyrs, crowded off the lists or forgotten even in their own churches. Others, like Anastasia who died on December 25, had their day overshadowed later by a festival of greater importance and thus passed into relative oblivion.[6] The days of the martyrs, however, antedate the days of the apostles, and in the earliest calendars, the title "martyr" far outnumbers the title "saint."

In addition to the yearly observances, the early church also had a weekly cycle. Every Sunday was the Lord's Day and was a celebration of the resurrection. That is why, to this day, Sundays are never fast days, not even during Lent. Every Friday was a fast day in remembrance of the crucifixion, and there are traces of an early Wednesday fast in memory of our Lord's betrayal.

The calendar of the primitive church exhibits considerable Hebrew influence, though the Christian observances retained none of the Jewish meaning. This is not surprising since the disciples were Jews. The dates of Easter and Good Friday— the Pascha—were determined by the date of the Jewish Passover. Jesus went up to Jerusalem to eat the Passover with his disciples and it was while he was there that he was arrested and crucified. His body was hastily removed from the cross at sun-

---

[6] In the Roman Missal, St. Anastasia is commemorated at the second (*Aurora*) mass on Christmas with a collect, a secret and a postcommunion collect.

down on Good Friday so that it might not hang there on the Great, or Paschal, Sabbath which began at six o'clock in the evening. His resurrection occurred on the first day of the week "when the sabbath was past." The date of Pentecost was seven weeks later at the time of the Jewish Feast of the Weeks which was, in our Lord's time, a spring harvest festival.

For the early Christians, too, as for the Jews, the day began at evening. The days in the creation story had been counted "evening and morning." [7] The sabbath was to be celebrated "from even unto even." [8] This practice persisted in the church for seven centuries and continues in the Roman Catholic church in the vigils which precede the major festivals. An early service of this sort is described in Acts 20:7-12, where the "first day" begins at sundown and St. Paul preaches until midnight and the sermon is followed by the breaking of bread. The service ended at daybreak.

The seven-day week is another Jewish contribution. In the ancient world weeks were of varying lengths. The Greeks divided their months into three ten-day periods. The Roman week had eight days. The seven-day week, which the Christian church carried all over the world, was of West Asian origin and was little known in Jesus' day except among the Jews and Jewish colonies. Within this week, Tuesday and Thursday were kept by pious Jews as fast days; Saturday was kept as the holy day.[9] The Christians fasted on Wednesdays and Fridays and kept Sunday as the holy day. The use of different days and the special significance attached to them emphasized for Jewish converts the complete change that was necessary in embracing the new faith. For a time, a Judaizing party (Ebionites) within the church tried to maintain the Sabbath side by side with Sunday, but the effort failed.

[7] Gen. 1:5ff.
[8] Lev. 23:32.
[9] Luke 18:12.

At the beginning of the fourth century, the church year included the Pascha, commemorative of both the passion and resurrection; Pentecost, commemorative of the descent of the Holy Spirit; Epiphany, commemorative of the manifestation of Christ in his birth and baptism; the days of local martyrs; Sundays as commemorations of the resurrection; fasting on Fridays and perhaps Wednesdays; the seven-day week with the days beginning at sundown.

The Edict of Toleration in 313, however, resulted in profound changes in the nature and character of the church. Now, for the first time, it was able to operate openly and without fear of persecution. It could build churches and basilicas, relax the rigorous examination and scrutiny of catechumens, hold public services and processions, and attempt to recover its historic places. It was this last effort, very prominent in the fourth century, that was most important in stimulating the further development of the church year. Pilgrimages to holy places— the site of the crucifixion, of the sepulchre, of the last supper, of the ascension, of the nativity—and the erection of basilicas on many of these historic spots gave rise to special services in special places on special days. The various processions and services held in Jerusalem in the fourth century are described in detail by a Christian woman from Gallicia who had made a pilgrimage there.[10] It was only natural that she and other Christians should return home and encourage the adaptation and imitation of these ceremonies. This was especially true in Rome. Here the bishop and his clergy were soon proceeding to the Church of St. Mary Major at midnight on Christmas Eve to say mass beside a reproduction of the crèche in Bethlehem. In addition to these replicas, Rome had, as did other

[10] The English translation, as well as the Latin text, of the *Peregrinatio Aetheriae* appears in L. Duchesne, *Christian Worship* (London: S.P.C.K., 1949). She is believed to have made her pilgrimage near the end of the fourth century.

Christian centers, its own holy places with their own apostolic traditions, real or legendary.

Relics also played a part in the development of the church year. Churches and shrines in places far removed from the Holy Land attained an increased, if second hand, importance by the translation of relics to their altars. Helen, mother of the Emperor Constantine, believed that she had found the true cross. She brought part of it to Rome and converted her Sessorian Palace into the Church of the Holy Cross in Jerusalem. It became at once the site of the Good Friday devotions of the Roman Catholic church. Other relics gave special significance to other churches, and different services and calendars developed.[11] Some of these became general and found their way into the church year. In this process, the practice of the church of Rome, for the same reasons that gave it predominance in the West in other areas of church life, became in the course of time the accepted practice of Western Christianity.

A further development in the fourth century was the division of each of the three great ancient festivals. Before the century was over the Pascha had been divided into Easter and Good Friday; Epiphany had given birth to Christmas, and Pentecost to Ascension Day.[12] The development of Good Friday took place in Jerusalem and was directly connected with the Holy Week ceremonies which repeated the drama of the Passion at the historic places.

The Epiphany, always an important festival in the Eastern church, was observed in Gaul and in Spain in the fourth century, but apparently never at Rome as a festival of the birth

[11] The mind of fourth- (and fourteenth-) century man was not as skeptical of relics as we are. He asked little by way of authentication, and kings were often as gullible as peasants—and much better customers. From 1215 (The Fourth Lateran Council) the Roman Catholic church has threatened fraud with excommunication; but by 1215 most of the damage had been done.

[12] A. Alan McArthur, *The Evolution of the Christian Year* (London: S.C.M. Press, 1954). A scholarly discussion of the three "unitive" festivals and their division.

and baptism of our Lord. Instead, at some time before 336, December 25 was established as the festival of Jesus' birth. The date was chosen to sublimate the great pagan Roman festival of the Unconquered Sun (*Natalis solis invicti*) which took place at the winter solstice. Since the day, the month, even the year of the birth of Christ were not known, what more appropriate than to replace the Unconquered Sun with the birth of Jesus, Sun of Righteousness, at the time when the days began to lengthen again? Eventually both December 25 and January 6 were kept by both the Eastern and Western churches —the former, as the birth of our Lord; the latter, as the baptism of Christ in the East, and as the festival of the Magi (Three Kings) in the West.

Ascension Day was not separated from Pentecost until late in the fourth century in Asia Minor. Strangely, since it was the type of occasion that would have been ideal for liturgical re-en-actment, Etheria is silent about any Ascension Day celebration which was separated from Pentecost.[13] She mentions a service forty days after Easter, but it was in Bethlehem and was in commemoration of the Holy Innocents. The end of the century, however, found the two festivals separated in Antioch and Constantinople.

As the festivals were divided, so also the seasons of the church year developed. The only season already in existence before the fourth century was the Easter season of seven weeks. By the end of the fourth century Lent was firmly established. It developed in two directions. There was in the primitive church a fast preceding the Pascha. It was not, however, a Good Friday fast since Good Friday was not celebrated, though some Christians began their fast on Friday. Most of the faithful fasted on Saturday, and the fast was not broken until the

---

[13] Etheria is the name given the author of the *Peregrinatio* (cf. footnote 10, *supra*). She is also called Sylvia.

Eucharist, celebrated at about 3 A.M. Easter morning. Gradually this fast was extended, first to the forty hours our Lord spent in the tomb, then to six days by the early third century. This part of Lent, which we know as Holy Week, seems to have developed as a preparation for Easter. The rest of Lent derives from the ancient practice of preparing catechumens for baptism at Easter. There was a series of lectures and scrutinies or examinations which began about six weeks before Easter. All candidates were further expected to fast the forty days preceding the Pascha, as our Lord had fasted before beginning his ministry.[14] The penitents (those under discipline) also fasted in preparation for their reconciliation at Eastertime. After the Edict of Toleration in 313 the severity of these exercises began to be relaxed, and the period of fasting was transferred to all the faithful.

The length of Lent varied, too. At first the fast seems to have begun on the Monday of the sixth week before Easter. This *Quadragesima* is referred to in the fifth canon of the Council of Nicaea in 325. By the end of the fourth century it had been extended to seven weeks in Egypt. In Jerusalem, Etheria found an eight-week Lent with all Saturdays except Saturday in Holy Week, and all Sundays, excepted from the fast. The exception of Sundays spread as Lent became more widely observed, and, to bring the total number of days in the fast back to forty, the days from Ash Wednesday on in the seventh week before Easter were added. The tendency to extend Lent still farther is evidenced by the three pre-Lenten Sundays (Septuagesima, Sexagesima and Quinquagesima) which, in the modern Roman Catholic church, are hardly distinguishable from Lent. Caesarius of Arles prescribed a pre-Lent fast for monks in the sixth

---

[14] Matt. 4:2; Luke 4:2. See also the forty days spent by Moses on Sinai (Exod. 24:18; Deut. 9:9) and by Elijah on his journey to the Mount of God (1 Kings 19:8).

century, and there were other parts of the church in which a preparatory season was customary.

As Lent eventually developed into a period of preparation before Easter, so Advent developed into a period of preparation before Christmas. In Spain, where the Epiphany was observed in the fourth century, it was preceded by a three-week period of fasting and daily church attendance beginning on December 17. It spread to Gaul and Italy and was transferred to Christmas. As with Lent, so the length of Advent varied. In Gaul, it began as early as St. Martin's Day (November 11) and lasted six weeks. In Spain and Italy, it included five weeks. Advent was finally settled at four weeks in Rome, though the lessons for the last Sunday after Trinity in both Lutheran and Anglican use are reminiscent of the centuries when Advent was a longer season.

Around Christmas there clustered certain holydays which depend literally upon Christmas for their dates. The Circumcision of our Lord was eight days later on January 1.[15] The Presentation of our Lord (also called Candlemas, or the Purification of the Virgin Mary) was forty days after Christmas, February 2.[16] The Annunciation, nine months earlier, was March 25.[17] The Nativity of John the Baptist, who was six months older than Jesus, was set at June 24.[18] The wisdom of the conflation of a literal principle with a liturgical one is open to question. Certainly both the annunciation and the nativity of John the Baptist are more at home during Advent from a liturgical point of view.

With the acceptance of the new festivals, and the completion

[15] Luke 2:21. The counting is Roman style, including both the first and last days. For us, an octave (eight days) is one week later.
[16] Lev. 12:1-4.
[17] Luke 1:36.
[18] Luke 1:36. The reason it is June 24 instead of June 25 is due to the Roman system of reckoning. December 25 is the eighth day before the kalends of January; June 24 is the eighth day before the kalends of July.

of Lent and Advent, the church followed for half of each year a cycle which recalled the life of Christ: his advent, nativity, manifestation, suffering, crucifixion, death, resurrection and ascension, and the descent of the Holy Spirit on Pentecost. The cycle was not entirely complete,[19] but it was, and is still, the high semester of the church year, including the major festivals and repeating perennially for the Christian the principal events in God's scheme of redemption.

The word "events" deserves emphasis. Festivals commemorating doctrines of the church and those of the Virgin Mary are of later origin.[20] Trinity Sunday, for instance, after which many north European missals numbered the Sundays in the second half of the year,[21] was not officially accepted until the fourteenth century, although it had been a popular festival in many places for several centuries previous. After 1570, when the Roman Missal received its final form under Pius V, the Sundays in the latter half of the church year were numbered as they had been numbered at Rome—after Pentecost. This second half of the year was devoted to the Christian life, and the application to it of the lessons of the life and teaching of our Lord and the Apostles.

This church year has evolved slowly over many centuries under the guidance of the Holy Spirit. Within its framework it provides for the annual review of the great events of God's work in time in the person of his Son, and of the meaning of those events for God's people. The church has always impoverished itself when it has abandoned the church year, or

---

[19] For instance, the fourth, fifth and sixth Sundays after the Epiphany still evidence an incompleteness of this part of the church year by repeating items proper to the third Sunday.

[20] Except those festivals of the Virgin Mary which were originally observed as festivals of our Lord, e.g., the Presentation and the Annunciation.

[21] The Sarum Missal and the missals of dioceses in Germany and Scandinavia, from which the Anglicans and Lutherans took their use, numbered the Sundays after Trinity. The numbering after Pentecost is not only more ancient, but Pentecost is an event from which other events can be dated. Trinity is not.

attempted to reconstruct it. In the sixteenth century the conservative reformers were aware of this fact and retained the
church year, eliminating only those festivals which were felt
to be unwarranted on the basis of the teachings of Christ. The
more radical reformers discarded the historic year. In Puritan
England and Calvinistic Scotland, from which many of the
early American settlers came, the church year was regarded with
suspicion as "popery." The result has been that Protestant
America, excepting the liturgical churches, has had an impoverished background. Attempts have been made to supply
the want by such "festivals" as Rally Day, World Peace Sunday,
Race Relations Sunday, Brotherhood Sunday, Festival of the
Christian Home (Mother's Day), Rural Life Sunday, Children's Day, Labor Sunday, etc.[22] Were these related to the
historic church year, some of them could be acceptable, but
their dates bear little or no reference to the church year and
fall on different Sundays in different years. The date of World
Peace Sunday is determined by Armistice Day (November 11);
Race Relations Sunday by Lincoln's Birthday (February 12);
Brotherhood Sunday by Washington's Birthday (February 22);
the Christian Home (second Sunday in May); Rural Life Sunday (third Sunday in May) although Rogate, on which it sometimes falls, would be more acceptable. A glance at most of
these titles will indicate the difference in orientation between
the historic church year and its festivals and attempts to manu-
facture a substitute. The attempt to relate the problems of the
day to the message of God is not irrelevant, but it is not the
same thing as relating the redemptive process of God to the
problems of the day.

[22] For a complete round see Clarence Seidenspinner, *Great Protestant Festivals*
(New York: Henry Schuman, 1952).

3.

ANCIENT SERVICE BOOKS
AND CALENDARS

The history of the development of the church year is a highly
technical and complicated study. Its sources are the ancient
sacramentaries, calendars, missals, canons (decrees) of general
councils, and occasional papal bulls. Most of these materials
were prepared in monastic *scriptoria,* or copy rooms, by monks
who devoted their entire lives to the copying of documents and
the making of books. The word "books" is likely to be mis-
leading to twentieth-century readers who naturally think in
terms of bound and printed volumes. The books were hand
lettered and were often unbound sheets or rolls of parchment.
Because of the time and labor involved in their preparation,
they were both rare and expensive. But because of the quality
of materials used, they were also quite durable, and a surprising
number of them have survived.

There was, however, a different code of ethics among
medieval copyists, and because of the conscienceless manner in
which they often added to and changed older manuscripts
rather than go to the trouble of writing completely new ones,
each surviving document has had to be carefully studied on the
basis of its own internal evidence and a careful reconstruction
made of its original form and subsequent change. This has
required scholars with highly technical knowledge not only of
ancient languages, abbreviations, and methods of reckoning

time, but also of local church history and customs. This has been particularly necessary in order to date the documents and to locate their geographical provenance.

In the first few centuries, the only books we know of which were used in the church were portions of the Bible. The rest of the material was in a more or less fluid state and was said by the priest, his assistants and the people, either extemporaneously or from memory. This does not mean that everything was composed on the spur of the moment. There were many phrases and sentences that were already becoming traditional, and younger ministers learned them and patterned their prayers, for instance, after the models of their elders. The people answered with their alleluias, Kyrie eleisons or amens —simple responses which could be easily memorized.

Among the first written items were the lists of people, both living and dead, for whom prayers were to be offered at the services. Written at first on two wax-covered tablets, hinged and folded, these formed the diptych. The next oldest "book" was probably the *comes,* or companion, to the lessons. At first the lessons were read continuously, the reader starting where he had stopped at the last service and continuing until the bishop gave him a signal to stop. This method of reading is known as *lectio continua.* But this lack of order was soon replaced by the reading of a set portion of Scripture at each service. It then became necessary to know where to begin and where to end each lesson, and an index showing the first and last words of each lesson was prepared.[1] This is the source of

---

[1] This was also known later as a capitulary, an example of which follows:
The first sonnenday in aduent
    Rom xiij c   we knowen this time
                   ende. in the lord Ihs Ct
    Matheu xxj c   whanne ihs cam nighe
                   ende. osanna in high thingis.
First is written a clause of the begynnynge of the pistil & gospel, & a clause of the endynge thereof.
This capitulary is in the British Museum. Cf. William Maskell, *Monumenta Ritualia Ecclesiae Anglicanae* (London: William Pickering, 1846), vol. I, p. liv.

the word "pericope" which means "a portion cut off." But, since books other than the Bible were sometimes used for lessons (such as the lives of the saints, martyrologies, sermons and homilies of noted preachers) a companion (*comes*) to the lessons appeared, which indicated the lessons for each service. It was only one further step to the preparation of separate books for the lessons, which avoided the necessity for looking them up elsewhere. So the epistles were written out in an *epistolarium,* the gospels in an *evangelarium,* and a complete set of lessons in the *lectionarium.*

In the fourth century the prayers began to be written, too, and to circulate and become more or less uniform in the churches. That this practice was recent and upsetting to the church is indicated by the action of a synod at Hippo (North Africa) in 393, which forbade "anyone to use written-out prayers of other churches till he has shown his copy to the more learned brethren." [2]

In the writing of the prayers and other parts of the liturgy, the complete services did not appear in any one book, but separate books were prepared for each minister's part. Thus the bishop or priest had his book, the sacramentary or *euchologion;* the deacon had his, the *diakonikon;* the choir had theirs—an antiphonary, *liber gradualis, liber responsalis* or *psalterium.* In the early church there was nothing corresponding to the present missal, common prayer, or common service book, in which the complete service appears in one book in all its parts. Books like these had to await the day when the multiplication of copies would become less expensive and less laborious.

The most important books are the three great sacramentaries of the ancient western church—the Leonine, Gelasian and Gregorian. Though bearing the names of famous bishops of Rome: Leo the Great (440-461), Gelasius I (492-496), and

---

[2] Adrian Fortescue, *The Mass* (London: Longmans, Green, 1917), p. 114.

Gregory the Great (590-604), the real identity of their com-
pilers is not known, and the date of their appearances can only
be approximated.

The Leonine Sacramentary, which is the oldest of the three,
was probably prepared in Rome at the end of the fifth or the
beginning of the sixth century. There is only one manuscript
copy in existence (at Verona) and that is defective. The section
from the middle of December to the middle of April is missing.
It is an anthology of masses.

The Gelasian Sacramentary was also prepared at Rome,
probably in the seventh century. The oldest manuscript, now
in the Vatican Library, was written near the end of the seventh
century for use in the Abbey of St. Denis in Paris. Other copies
have been found at St. Gall and Rheinau, and all three have
been collated. The Gelasian Sacramentary is divided into three
parts. The first part contains masses for Sundays and holydays
from Christmas Eve (the beginning of the church year in the
seventh century) to Pentecost. The second contains lessons,
prayers, etc., for saints' days as well as five masses for Advent,
which was not yet well enough established to be included in
the first part. The third part contains masses for any Sunday,
votive masses, the canon of the mass, and miscellaneous
blessings.

The Gregorian Sacramentary comes also from Rome and
dates from the eighth century. It was introduced into Gaul
(France) by Charlemagne in 791. The oldest copy, found at
Monte Cassino, dates from the eighth century; two others date
from the ninth. It is in four parts: the order of the mass,
ordination, the propers for the year, and a collection of blessings, prayers and votive masses.

Because of the pre-eminence of the Roman church in the
West, these books gradually supplanted other sacramentaries

and service books, a few of which are known, including the Gothic Missal (Autun, seventh century), the Gallican Missal (Gaul, seventh century), the Lectionary of Luxeuil (Paris, seventh century), the Frankish Missal (France, end of the seventh century), the Stowe Missal (Ireland, eighth century), Mozarabic missals (Spain, seventh to eleventh centuries), Ambrosian missals (Milan, tenth century), the Bobbio Missal (northern Italy, seventh century), the Leofric Missal (Exeter, tenth century) and the Ravenna Roll—a fragment containing prayers in preparation for Christmas (northern Italy, unknown date). There are also a number of editions of the *Ordines Romani,* books of rubrical directions for services, beginning with the eighth century.

All of these service books are important because they indicate by their provisions what services were held in different periods of the church's development. Many of the later ones included calendars.

The earliest calendars used in the church were probably the diptychs of the living, of the dead, and of the local bishops, which were originally read at stated places in the service.[3] In time it became impossible to read at each service the entire list of distinguished members, and the church adopted a scheme of commemorating them on the date of their deaths. Lists of the dead with the dates of their martyrdom came to be known as martyrologies in the West; menologies in the East. They were prepared for local use at first, and gradually included the festivals and fasts of the church as well as the anniversaries of the martyrs. The calendars were quite simple, containing the date, the name of the festival or martyr, perhaps a word or two of description, and occasionally an extra-ecclesiastical comment. The martyrologies were quite extensive, including the

---

[3] This reading took place during the canon of the mass, from which practice the word "canonize" got its meaning of "making one a saint."

circumstances of the martyrdom and sometimes a brief life of
the martyr.

The earliest extant calendars date from the fourth century
and a comparative study of them is important in tracing the
introduction and spread of festivals, seasons and holydays from
time to time and place to place. Important calendars are the
Philocalian (fourth century, Rome), the Hieronymian Martyrology (sixth century, France), the Martyrology of Silos (seventh
century, Spain), Coptic calendars (seventh to ninth centuries,
Africa), the Menology of Constantinople (eighth century), the
Menology of Basil (tenth century, Constantinople), the
Martyrology of Bede (eighth century, England), of Ado (ninth
century, France), of Usuardus (ninth century, France), of
Rabanus Maurus (ninth century, Germany), and of Notker
Balbulus (ninth century, Switzerland). After the eighth century, when calendars began to appear in missals, calendars are
available from Rome, Bologna, Sens, Corbie, Lodeve, Win-
chester, Durham, Auxerre, Mainz, Werden, Cologne, Essen,
Strassburg, Treves and Worcester.

All of these calendars of the Western church appeared in
Latin and used the Roman system of reckoning time. Thus a
line from an eleventh-century calendar reads for October 31:

x   C   ii Kl   Sci quinanimay — Uigilia

The first column "x" is the golden number which reconciled
the solar and lunar years, and was of use in calculating the
date of Easter. The numbers ran from one to 19 and each
day's golden number was 11 less than the previous day's. The
second item "C" indicates the day of the week. Each year had
a Sunday letter, and each day was lettered A to G. The "ii Kl"
means the second day before the kalends of November. The
Roman system counts dates backwards from the next kalends,
nones or ides. The kalends is always the first of the next month.
The ides are the fifteenth of March, May, July and October, and

the thirteenth in all other months. The nones are always the
ninth day before the ides (both days included), the seventh of
March, May, July and October; the fifth in all other months.
"Ii Kl" is the day before November 1. The legend reads "All
Saints' Vigil" which is the eve of All Saints' Day, or Hal-
lowe'en.

In a twelfth-century calendar an entry reads:

      vi   E   x Kl   Scti Mathei apti eugle   Alb

Again "vi" is the golden number; "E" the day of the week;
"x Kl" is the tenth day before the kalends (of October, in this
case), both days included, which would make it the twenty-first
of September. The occasion is St. Matthew, Apostle, Evangelist.
"Alb" specifies white stoles and paraments. Calendars sometimes contained almanac references such as *sol in Scorpio, sol
in Libram, dies mala* (unlucky day), *dies caniculares* (dog
day).

As time went by, these once simple calendars became highly
complex and tremendously overloaded with festivals. On the
frame of the church year were hung hundreds of festivals of
new saints, the Virgin Mary, and doctrines of the church, until
there was scarcely a day without a commemoration. On most
days there were a number of saints; there had to be, in order to
accommodate the 2,000 of them to a 365-day year. Not all of
them were commemorated throughout the church[4] and many
that were not given the same dignity everywhere. St. Mark, for
instance, was much more important in Venice, where he was
the patron saint, than at Rome. A complicated system of
rankings rose to establish a protocol. Festivals were ranked
from doubles of the first class down to simples.[5] Added to this
already complex system were numerous octaves and vigils.[6]

[4] In the Bamberg Missal, for instance, St. Kunnegund, German empress who
died in 1040, is commemorated on several days, one of which has an octave.
Her appearance at all in calendars other than German is very rare.
[5] Present rankings in the Roman Catholic church are:

This multiplication of commemorations, especially of saints, also resulted in a multiplication of masses. The breviary, which contained the daily offices, grew eventually to four thick volumes and a common complaint, voiced in the preface to the *Book of Common Prayer* (1549), was that it took longer to find out what was to be read than to read it after it was found! And if the clergy were baffled, what of the laity? For the layman, the mass became a spectacle at which his status was reduced to that of a passive observer. Without a book in his hand (and often unable to read one even if he had had one), he no longer knew when the ancient spontaneous responses of alleluia, Kyrie eleison and amen ought to be made.

In the Reformation, the calendar was simplified by a return in general to a Scriptural basis. The saints' days retained were for the most part those of New Testament saints. The only festivals of the Virgin Mary retained were those which were really festivals of our Lord. Classification of festivals was reduced to a simple major or minor, or red letter and black letter. Accompanying this reform was a great simplification of service books which, coinciding as it did with the invention of printing with movable type, enabled the laity to participate to a degree never before possible in the history of the church.

The purpose of the reformers was to return the church year to its original purpose—that of recalling perennially the events of the life of Christ and to relate those events to the life of

Double first class	e.g., Easter
Double second class	St. James
Double major	Conversion of St. Paul
Double	St. Bruno
Semidouble	St. Hilary
Simple	St. Praxedes

The only festival retained by the Protestant church that was not a double of the first or second class was the Conversion of St. Paul.

[6] An octave is the eighth day after a festival counting both days. At first only Easter, Pentecost and (in the East) Epiphany had octaves. Vigils were originally night services preceding a festival; later they became fasts on the preceding day. Only Easter, Pentecost and (in the East) Epiphany had vigils at first.

the believer. They sought to restore to the church year its original meaning, rather than permit it to continue as a somewhat mechanical round of feast and fast. In doing this, they recovered its Christocentricity, a feature which had become as much obscured in the calendar as it had in liturgy, government and doctrine. Thus the calendar of the Protestant church is not a new one of post-Reformation provenance. With minor exceptions,[7] it is the calendar of the Christian church[8] of ancient times as observed in the West.

[7] Reformation Day (October 31) in Lutheran use; the Name of Jesus (August 7) in Anglican use.

[8] No attempt is made here to deal with the calendar of the Eastern church which, after the fourth century, developed in its own way. Many festivals are the same; the dates are often different.

4.

THE CHURCH YEAR AND
THE SERVICE

In the Eastern church, the liturgy remained the same week after week. In the Western church, it was related to the church year through the use of variable parts inserted in a constant framework. The variable parts are called the propers (*propria*). The framework consisted of two parts. The first was the Liturgy of the Word, or Mass of the Catechumens, which ended after the Gospel for the day. At this point in the primitive church, all but the baptized were dismissed. The second part was the Liturgy of the Upper Room, or Mass of the Faithful, which began with the offertory and included the Eucharist (Holy Communion).

The Liturgy of the Word was characterized by psalmody and lessons. As time went by, certain psalms and passages of Scripture came to be associated with certain Sundays and festivals. On Christmas, the gospel story of the birth of Christ was the gospel for the day. And it would have been unthinkable to have omitted reading on Pentecost the account of the first Christian Pentecost from the Book of Acts. The psalms, which eventually took the title of introit, gradual, and tract, likewise soon formed stated associations with particular occasions. The brief prayer called the collect, which was said before the first lesson, was quite likely to contain some reference either to the occasion or to the teaching of the day. In these variable parts of the Liturgy of the Word the church made real the cycle of the life of Christ and the life of the Christian.

The second part of the service, the Liturgy of the Upper Room, remained the same Sunday after Sunday for a longer period. But eventually seasonal and festival adaptations began to be made. The oldest, and the one retained by the reformers, was the use of a proper preface to relate the communion of the day to the church year. Later, in medieval times, the offertory psalm and secret and postcommunion prayer became additional variable features.

Of all the Protestant churches, the Lutheran church retained most of these variables features, including the introit, collect, an optional Old Testament lesson, the epistle, gradual, gospel and proper prefaces.[1] The Anglican church retained only the collect, epistle, gospel and proper prefaces, though Cranmer's First Prayer Book of Edward VI (1549) did provide introits which were dropped in 1552. In the lesser services, such as matins and vespers, the Lutheran reformers retained the entire body of variable material including psalms, lessons, collects, antiphons, invitatories, responsories and canticles.[2] Through the use of these variable parts of the services, while the framework remains constant, the outward appearance of the liturgy will be somber on Good Friday and joyful on Easter.

THE INTROIT

The first hymnal of the Christian church was the Book of Psalms, and the earliest chants of the church are all psalms, parts of psalms, or texts written on the model of the psalms.

---

[1] There is some slight variety in Lutheran use of the offertory psalm and there is no reason why a series of offertories and postcommunion collects should not some day be restored. The reformers did not object to the idea, but to the content of the then existing series.

[2] The variable features of the lesser services, developed for daily use, cannot be examined here.

The origin of the use of a psalm to open the liturgy is not known. One Roman tradition ascribes it to Pope Celestine I (422-432),[3] who ordered that "the 150 Psalms of David be sung by all antiphonally before mass." Another tradition credits Pope Gelasius I (492-496).

The fourth and fifth centuries were the heyday of processions. In Rome on certain days masses were said at certain churches which were known as "stational churches." [4] The clergy and people assembled and went in procession to the stational church of the day. En route, psalms were sung, the introit psalm being sung as the procession entered the stational church. When processions went out of style, the accustomed introit psalm continued to be sung—or rather enough of it to cover the entry of the clergy. When they were in their places, a sign was given to the choir to stop the psalm and proceed immediately with the *Gloria Patri.* Thus the introit shrank from a complete psalm to one verse preceded by an antiphon. This was followed by the *Gloria Patri* and then the antiphon was repeated.[5] Thus we have the curious situation that, on some occasions, the antiphon is longer than the psalm.[6]

The normal or regular introit consists of an antiphon taken from the same psalm as the introit psalm, followed by the first verse of the psalm; or when the antiphon itself is the first verse of the psalm, followed by the second verse of the same psalm. The introit for Sexagesima (antiphon Ps. 44:23-26; Ps. 44:1) is an example of the first type. The introit for the

[3] Dates following the names of popes are those of their incumbency.
[4] In this century, the stational procession and mass have been restored in Rome and its suburbs. Eighty-nine masses in forty-five stational churches are presently celebrated in Rome and its suburbs during the church year.
[5] An antiphon is a verse, usually from a psalm, which seems to have once been a people's refrain after each verse of the psalm. Eastern in origin, it was introduced to the West by St. Ambrose of Milan in the fourth century.
[6] The verse of the introit marked *Ps* is the psalm verse. All that precedes is the antiphon. Cf. Sexagesima where the antiphon has three verses, the psalm one.

First Sunday in Advent (antiphon Ps. 25:1-3; Ps. 25:4) is an example of the second. Irregular introits are those which take their antiphons from other parts of the Bible or even from extra-scriptural sources. The introit for the Fourth Sunday in Advent (antiphon Isa. 45:8; Ps. 19:1) is an example of the former. The introit for the Epiphany, beginning "Behold the Lord, the Ruler, hath come," is an example of the latter.

Since the introit is the first item in the service and its text begins the day's worship, Sundays were often named popularly after the opening words of their introits: *Invocabit, Reminiscere, Oculi, Laetare* and *Judica* in Lent, and the Sundays after Easter.

THE COLLECT

The second variable feature of the service is the collect for the day, which is a brief prayer following the *Gloria in excelsis* and preceding the first lesson. Its origin may also lie in the ancient stational services at Rome. The people gathered at a church before proceeding to the stational church of the day. This first assembly was known as the *collecta,* and the prayer said there before the procession set forth was the *oratio ad collectam.*[7] This prayer was then repeated after the stational church was reached and the introit and *Gloria* had been sung.

Or the word "collect" may refer to another ancient practice at this point in the service. Some scholars believe that in ancient times something like the following took place. Originally, the *Gloria in excelsis* was not sung at every service. but only at bishops' masses. After the *Gloria,* the bishop's salutation was and still is "Peace be with you" which continues the theme of "on earth peace, good will to men." Then another of the clergy, a deacon, made the bid to prayer. But instead of a general bid, he added something specific to be prayed for.

[7] Adrian Fortescue, *The Mass, op. cit.,* pp. 244-45.

There followed a moment of silence during which the people made their private petitions, and then the bishop "collected" the petitions of the people in a brief summary prayer which in time became known as the collect.[8]

However the title came to be, the collects form one of the oldest features of the service. The sixth-century Leonine Sacramentary furnishes the oldest ones,[9] and more than three-fourths of the collects are from the seventh-century Gelasian Sacramentary, in the preparation of which the older Leonine was undoubtedly used. A few others are from the Gregorian Sacramentary.[10] Nine-tenths of the collects appointed for Sundays and holydays have been in Christian use for more than twelve hundred years, and the newest are as old as the age of the Reformation.

The collects, however, have not commended themselves to the church solely because of their antiquity. They are remarkable for the terse manner in which they express the desires of God's people before his throne. The older the collect, the shorter it is likely to be, expressing only one clearly-defined petition. For this purpose the Latin language was peculiarly well fitted and, while our English translations have caught the spirit and thought of the originals and are often literary gems in their own right, there is a certain lapidary quality about the Latin which cannot be reproduced. The collect for Jubilate requires only 29 Latin words in the Leonine Sacramentary; in English it requires 63!

The structure of the collect normally includes an address,

---

[8] This ancient form of prayer, still very effective, survives in the Bidding Prayer. The deacon says "Let us pray for the whole Christian church. . . ." There follows a moment of silent prayer and then a collect for the church. The Bidding Prayer is of further interest because it is the germ of the Lutheran General Prayer and, next to the Lord's Prayer, probably the oldest form of corporate prayer surviving in the Christian church.

[9] Jubilate, and the Fourth, Eighth, Ninth, Twelfth and Thirteenth Sundays after Trinity.

[10] Cf. pp. 29-30, *supra*.

an ascription which is usually the basis for the petition, the petition itself and sometimes a reason for it, and the final clause "through Jesus Christ" with which all collects close. The ancient collects are addressed to God the Father; some later ones to God the Son.[11]

The collect is used not only on its appointed Sunday or festival but also at all services throughout the remainder of the week until vespers on Saturday. This use serves to bind the ordinary days to the liturgy and to the church year.

THE LESSONS

The first book used in the services of the church was the Bible. Initially it was, of course, the Old Testament. The reading of the Law and the Prophets was a feature of primitive Christian worship taken over from the synagogue worship with which many of the first Christians were familiar. Later, as New Testament writings became available, they were added. The number of lessons was not fixed. At one time there appear to have been as many as five: Law, Prophets, Epistle, Acts and Gospel. By the fifth century, this had been reduced to three: an Old Testament lesson, an epistle and a gospel. This was true of both the Eastern and Western church. Since the seventh century, however, the Western use at Rome has been only an epistle and a gospel. The other Western rites—Gallican, Mozarabic and Ambrosian—continued to have three.

The basis upon which certain lessons were selected for particular days is unknown. If there once was a basis, it has become so overlaid with later modifications that it has become indistinguishable. For some Sundays and festivals the reason is clear enough, and this is true generally of the first half of the church year. But the choices for Sundays during the second

[11] Cf. the collect for Thursday in Holy Week, written in 1264 by Thomas Aquinas for the then-new festival of Corpus Christi.

half of the year often appear to have neither rhyme nor reason. There have been many ingenious attempts to explain them, but the best that can be offered is an occasional conjecture.

Partly because of this there have been many attempts to provide new lectionaries on rational principles. Some of these have appeared in the Lutheran church; others in free churches which have approached the construction of a lectionary *de novo*. But none have succeeded in commending themselves as replacements for the historic western series, much of which goes back to the sixth century or before.[12]

In reading the lessons, the first and earliest Christian practice was to read the Bible through in course, that is, consecutively, beginning where the reader of the previous service had stopped. The lections were quite long and the reading was continued until a signal was received to stop. Gradually set portions came to be read at each service and the first and last words of each lection were noted. This was particularly necessary since there were no chapter and verse divisions to serve as guides.[13] This was the pericope. In time the epistles were written out in the *epistolarium,* a book presented at his ordination to the subdeacon who read the epistle at the service; and the gospels were written out in the *evangelarium,* a book presented at his ordination to the deacon, who read the gospels.

THE EPISTLE

Strictly speaking, an epistle is a portion of one of the books of the New Testament between Acts and Revelation. Liturgically, however, it is the lesson which precedes the gospel at the service, even though it may come from Acts (as on Pentecost), from Revelation (as on All Saints' Day), or from the Old

---

[12] S. Beissel, *Entstehung der Perikopen des Römischen Messbuches* (Freiburg, 1907). He thinks that many of the lessons may go back to the time of Pope Damasus (366-384).

[13] Verse divisions in the English Bible, for instance, date only from 1560.

Testament (as on Ash Wednesday). The people sit to hear it, as they do for all lessons except the gospel. In medieval churches, which were often furnished with two ambos,[14] the epistle and other lessons (except the gospel) were read from the south ambo. Today, though churches are no longer built with ambos, when the epistle is read from the altar it is read from the south side.[15] The reading of the epistle was the privilege of the subdeacon from the seventh century in the West. Before then it had been the duty of a lector (reader), one of the minor orders of clergy which disappeared.[16]

In medieval times, the epistle was chanted or intoned—a practice continued in early liturgical Protestantism, with permission for reading, however, in cases where it could not be intoned. In time, however, it became customary in many Protestant churches for the lessons to be read even in services which were otherwise chanted.

THE GOSPEL

The gospel, from one of the first four books of the New Testament, has always been the final lesson. It is the culmination of all the other lessons, containing the words and deeds of our Lord and occupying the place of honor at the end of the "procession" of Scripture. In many liturgies, this place of honor has been further heightened by additional ceremonies such as processions, lights, incense, prayers, kisses and signs of the cross. Its reading is bracketed by the responses *Gloria tibi* (Glory be to thee, O Lord) and *Laus tibi* (Praise be to thee, O Christ). In contrast to the other lessons which the people hear while seated, the gospel is heard standing.

[14] An ambo was an elevated reading desk or lectern with steps. In churches with only one ambo, the epistle was read from a lower step, the gospel from the top.

[15] The south side is the right side as one faces the altar which is, architecturally and liturgically, the east end.

[16] There were seven orders of clergy in the ancient church: *ostiarius* (doorkeeper), lector (reader), exorcist, acolyte, subdeacon (epistle), deacon (gospel) and priest.

In ancient times, the gospel was read from the north ambo, and later from the north side of the altar. It was read by the lector, and after that order disappeared, by the deacon. Next to the role of celebrant at communion, the reading of the gospel was the highest privilege in the service. Like the epistle, it was chanted.

"In every part of Christendom enormous reverence was always shown to the book of the Gospels. The book was written with every possible splendour—sometimes entirely in gold or silver letters on vellum stained purple—and bound in gorgeous covers with carved ivory, metalwork, jewels. . . . The Gospel was often carried aloft in processions and was placed on a throne or altar, as presiding at synods. The meaning of all this is that the book was used as a symbol of our Lord Himself. It is certainly a suitable one. More than a statue or cross the book that contains his words may stand as a symbol of his presence." [17]

Inventories of church ornaments often carry entries such as "a booke of gospelles garnished and wrought with antique works of silver and gilte with an image of the crucifix with Mary and John, together 122 oz." In the Cathedral of Salisbury (England) there was a copy of the gospels ornamented with 20 sapphires, eight topazes, eight garnets, twelve pearls and other precious stones.[18]

THE GRADUAL

Between the epistle and the gospel, and maintaining the ancient alternation of Scripture and psalmody, is the chant called the gradual. It takes its name from the Latin word *gradus* or step, because it appears to have been sung from the step of the ambo from which the epistle had been read, and covered the action of moving from one ambo to the other for

---

[17] Fortescue, *op. cit.,* pp. 283-4.
[18] Maskell, *op. cit.,* vol. I, p. lii.

the gospel. It is one of the oldest parts of the service, known even to Tertullian (d.220) and Augustine (d.430). In their time the gradual was an entire psalm sung between the lessons.

With the reduction of the number of lessons to only two, the intervening chants were telescoped into one. So, today's gradual is the remnant of two separate chants, the first of which was once sung between the Old Testament lesson and the epistle, and the second of which was sung between the epistle and the gospel. The former of these was the true gradual; the latter was the alleluia, or during Lent, the tract. The texts of the graduals, like those of the introits, are usually from the psalms. There are occasional departures, such as the first, second and fifth Sundays after Easter—all of which have New Testament graduals; and Trinity Sunday, which has a gradual from the apocryphal Song of the Three Holy Children.

Primitively, the gradual was sung responsively; later by one voice, the deacon, until Gregory the Great suppressed this custom in 595. He observed that singing the gradual "led deacons to think more of their voices than of weightier things." The second part of the present gradual is either the alleluia or tract. On joyful days, alleluia is sung. The word alleluia, which Luther called "the perpetual voice of the church," is part of the Christian inheritance from Judaism, and occurs in many early liturgies. In the Eastern church, it is sung at all services; in Rome, it was sung at first only on Easter, but now replaces the second psalm between the epistle and gospel. There are three alleluias, the second of which has a musically prolonged final syllable called the *jubilus.* To this drawn out and complicated musical phrase, a verse is fitted, usually from Scripture and often from the psalms, though not always.[19] After this verse

---

[19] Cf. Pentecost, where the gradual proper is from Psalm 104, and the alleluia is the *Veni Sancte Spiritus.*

(*versus alleluiaticus*), the alleluia is sung for the third time.[20]

In penitential seasons, the alleluia is replaced by the tract. This is a fragment of the ancient second psalm. It was called the *psalmus tractus* because of the unbroken manner in which it was sung straight through by the cantor. Tracts replace alleluias from Septuagesima to Easter Eve.

Just as the addition of words to musical phrases at the end of alleluia (a process known as farsing) resulted in the alleluiatic verse, so it also resulted in the construction of sequences. These were metrical hymns, originally prose texts, which were used as mnemonic devices to recall the notes of the *jubilus.* They soon developed into independent compositions and became very popular and numerous, especially in northern Europe. They also became something of a problem, lengthening the service unnecessarily, and were often inferior to the rest of the liturgy in both form and content. The Council of Trent (1570) finally winnowed the hundreds of medieval sequences and retained only five—*Victimae paschali, Veni Sancte Spiritus, Lauda Sion, Stabat Mater,* and *Dies irae*—all of which are retained in Protestant hymnody as well as in current Roman use.

THE PROPER PREFACES

The only variable part of the Liturgy of the Upper Room remaining in general Protestant use is the proper preface. Following the *Sursum corda* (Lift up your hearts) the service continues with the *Vere dignum* (It is truly meet, right and salutary). Then in the Eastern church comes the anaphora, or great prayer of thanksgiving, which does not vary with the calendar, but begins with the creation and works its way slowly through the Old and New Testaments. In its place, the West-

---

[20] The arrangement is slightly different on the Sundays after Easter, when the pattern is a double alleluia, verse, alleluia, verse, alleluia.

ern church relates the communion to the particular day or season by means of a proper preface at this point in the service.[21]

Since this custom began (in the Leonine Sacramentary in the sixth century), the number of proper prefaces has shrunk with the passage of time. There were 267 proper prefaces in the Leonine, some of which seem to have been the means by which the celebrant gave vent to his personal feelings of the moment. The Gelasian Sacramentary has only 53; the Gregorian only 10, to which another has since been added.[22]

By means of these variable elements, the Western church adapts the service of the day to the church year and provides variety within a constant framework.

[21] This was true not only of the Roman, but of the Gallican and Mozarabic rites in the West.
[22] One for festivals of the Virgin Mary. Eleventh century.

5.

LITURGICAL COLORS

One of the more noticeable ways in which the church marks the changing seasons of its year is by a sequence of colors for altar, pulpit and lectern hangings, chasubles and stoles. For the comfort of all the good ladies of altar guilds who have been horror-stricken at the thought that the wrong colors were on the altar, it should be stated right at the outset that the use of particular colors on particular days is a relatively late development in the church. In the ancient church, the constant color appears to have been white, or possibly an unbleached white. The first clear reference to another color is to red for Pentecost, in the twelfth century.

Innocent III, who became pope in 1198, wrote a little treatise before that time in which he mentions a color sequence for the first time. For days of apostles and martyrs, and Pentecost, he specifies red. For Lent and Advent, the color was black. White was the normal color for days when no other color was specified in the first half of the year; green was the color for ordinary days after Pentecost. "Mitigations" or substitutions were permitted: yellow for green, violet for black, and scarlet for red. For All Saints' Day and the two festivals of the Holy Cross, a choice was allowed between red and white. A century later, the only change was that of violet instead of black for Advent and Lent.[1]

[1] A good treatise on liturgical colors in English remains to be written. The best available information is in Joseph Braun, S.J., *Die liturgischen Paramente in Gegenwart und Vergangenheit* (Freiburg im Breisgau: Herder, 1924), p. 38ff.

It is, of course, probable that Innocent III did not establish a color sequence, but that he simply reported what he had observed as the then use of the church in Rome. But the use of varying colors associated with different days and seasons was then a comparatively new idea. In the ancient church the finest vestments and hangings were used for the great days regardless of their color, and this practice continued for many centuries.[2] Many churches, especially the smaller ones, could not afford and did not have more than one or two colors. Thus the early systems were built on the available materials and there was no uniformity of use.

In England, where the dominant pre-Reformation use was that of Sarum (Salisbury), country churches used only white and red. Red was used for ordinary Sundays and days and on festivals of martyrs. During the Christmas season, on Easter through Whitsuntide, and on the days of the seven festivals which were not those of martyrs (the Conversion of St. Paul, the Presentation, the Annunciation, the Nativity of St. John the Baptist, the Transfiguration, St. Michael and All Angels, and All Saints), the color was white. The other colors were optional and depended on their availability: violet or purple for week days in Advent and Lent, green (or blue) for weekdays after Trinity Sunday.

In Ellwangen (Württemberg), seven colors were used: white, red, green, yellow, violet, black and ash gray. Yellow was used for green during the Trinity season. Ash gray was used—as it was used quite generally in France—for Ash Wednesday and sometimes for Lent up to Passion Sunday. In many parts of England, too, this division of colors within Lent

[2] Even after the present Roman use was established by Pius V in 1570, variant uses continued. A 1581 inventory of the church in Heilsberg (in East Prussia south of Königsberg) contains the following note: "1 brown chasuble to be worn on duplex feasts; 1 blue chasuble to be worn on semiduplex; 1 red chasuble to be worn on feria" (ordinary days).

was observed, with the color from Passion Sunday to Good
Friday being red. In the diocese of Bath and Wells (England),
blue was used in Advent and from Septuagesima to Passion
Sunday; white was used from Christmas to the First Sunday
after the Epiphany and on the First Sunday after Easter; red was
used from the octave of the Epiphany to Septuagesima and
from Passion Sunday to Advent.[3] In Lichfield, red was used
from Passion Sunday to Easter; white from Easter through
Trinity Sunday; black for Advent and Lent; green or blue for
the rest of the year. At Westminster Abbey, white was the use
from Advent to either Candlemas (February 2) or Septuagesima (whichever occurred first); reddish (*subrubens*) from
Septuagesima to the First Sunday in Lent; black for the first
four weeks of Lent; red for the last two weeks of Lent, through
Easter to Advent except Ascensiontide and Whitsuntide; yellow
or green might be used instead of red for Whitsuntide.

These and other medieval systems indicate chiefly the lack of
any uniform system. On Easter, white, red and green were used
in different places; Ascensiontide: white, red or green; Lent:
violet, black, white, gray, red; Advent: violet, blue, black, white;
Trinity Sunday: white, yellow, blue, violet, green, red! The
ordinary color for the long season after Pentecost might be
white, green, yellow, or red.[4]

Out of these variations evolved the Roman system set forth
in the sixteenth century by Pius V. White is used for all
festivals of our Lord, of all saints who were not martyrs, the
Christmas season to the octave of Epiphany, Easter Eve to the

---

[3] Vernon Staley, *Ceremonial of the English Church* (4th ed., rev.; London:
A. R. Mowbray, 1927). See also vols. I & II, *The Transactions of the St. Paul's
Ecclesiological Society.*

[4] A survival of ancient parish church use in Lutheran countries is the rather
permanent red or green paraments used in many rural Lutheran churches in
America down to the present generation. The Lutheran church orders of the
sixteenth century do not say much about colors. Pre-Reformation diocesan uses
continued, though there was more conformity to the Roman use in northern
Europe than in England. Cf. Braun, *op. cit.,* p. 729ff.

eve of Pentecost; red for festivals of the Holy Spirit and all martyrs; green for the long season after Pentecost, and from the octave of Epiphany to Septuagesima; violet for Advent and Lent, and Septuagesima to Ash Wednesday; black on Good Friday; and rose is permitted on Gaudete (the third Sunday in Advent) and Laetare (the fourth Sunday in Lent). Cloth of gold is permitted as a substitute for red, green and white; cloth of silver is allowed as a substitute for white.[5]

It was not long before the medieval mind began to make symbolic connections between the colors and the days on which they were used. Red, the color of blood and fire, was proper for martyrs' days and festivals of the Holy Ghost. Violet or black, colors of penance and mourning, were proper for Advent and Lent. Green, the color of nature, was proper for ordinary occasions. White, symbol of joy and purity, was reserved for the greatest festivals.

Mingled with the association of the colors with the days of the church year, was a secondary association of the colors with the particular service. This practice developed later and has been carried quite far in the present Roman use. Thus black is used for a funeral regardless of the color of the day; or white for a wedding. This resulted, for instance, in stoles of more than one color. In a Roman infant baptism, the priest wears a stole with the violet side showing until after the renunciation of Satan, whereupon he reverses the stole and wears it white side out for the remainder of the ceremony. This use of colors in association with particular services or parts of services marks a distinct difference between the present Lutheran use and Roman and Anglican use. In Lutheran use, the color of the

---

[5] Cf. Bruce Marshall, *The World, the Flesh and Father Smith* (Boston: Houghton Mifflin, 1945), p. 74. "He wore the vestments which Mother de la Tour had embroidered for him. Cloth of gold on one side, because cloth of gold could be used on all feasts and ferial days, and black on the other, because there were always requiems to be said."

day is used for all services of that day, regardless of the nature
of the ceremonies. For a burial or a wedding on the Monday
after Pentecost, a Lutheran minister would wear red.[6]

The Lutheran church continued the Roman use in general,
though it continued to use white throughout the Epiphany
season, and changed to green from Septuagesima to Lent,
whereas the Roman use changed to green at the octave of
Epiphany and to violet at Septuagesima. The present general
Lutheran use in America is:

White from Christmas Eve through the Epiphany season,
except St. Stephen and Holy Innocents; from vespers of Holy
Saturday to vespers of the Saturday before Pentecost; the
Transfiguration, Presentation, Annunciation and Visitation;
Trinity Sunday and its octave; St. Michael and All Angels.

Red from vespers of Saturday before Pentecost to vespers
of Saturday before Trinity Sunday; Reformation Day, All
Saints' Day, and the Sunday following; the days of all apostles,
evangelists, and martyrs except St. John; the dedication of a
church; the anniversary of a church; the festival of harvest and
days of thanksgiving.

Green from vespers of the Saturday before Septuagesima to
vespers of the Tuesday before Ash Wednesday; from vespers
of the First Sunday after Trinity to vespers of the Saturday
before Advent Sunday, except on festivals and days for which
there is some other appointment.

Violet from vespers of the Saturday before Advent Sunday
to vespers on Christmas Eve; from vespers of the Tuesday
before Ash Wednesday to vespers on Holy Saturday, except
Good Friday.

---

[6] This Lutheran use tends to tie all special occasions into the framework of
the church year. An idea of the Roman use may be gained from the following
examples: white is worn for sick communions, confirmations, marriages, churching of women, burial of baptized infants under seven years of age; violet for
exorcism, confession of the sick, extreme unction.

Black on Good Friday; a day of humiliation.

To which is added this rubric: "The celebration of the Holy Communion, the solemnization of Holy Matrimony and the Order for the Burial of the Dead shall not affect the proper color for day or season in use when these services may be held." [7]

In general, Anglican churches follow the Roman system in the use of liturgical colors.

In both Lutheran and Anglican churches, there was a general decline in liturgical observances during the seventeenth and eighteenth centuries, and it was not until the nineteenth century that there was a revival of interest and a restoration of many historic uses. The Oxford movement promoted the Roman color sequence in the Anglican church. In the Lutheran church, the revival was in large measure due to the work of Wilhelm Loehe, who organized a Society for Paramentics and trained many of his deaconesses at Neuendettelsau in ecclesiastical embroidery.[8] Today, there is a high degree of uniformity of use in both churches.

[7] *Common Service Book,* Music Edition, p. 293.
[8] See Henry E. Jacobs and John A. W. Haas, *The Lutheran Cyclopedia* (New York: Scribners, 1899), pp. 364-65.

6.

ADVENT

Since the eighth century, Advent has marked the beginning of the church year. The First Sunday in Advent is the Sunday occurring nearest, or upon, St. Andrew's Day, November 30. Advent Sunday may fall on any day between November 27 and December 3. And, while always including four Sundays, the season varies in length from 22 to 28 days from its variable beginning to its invariable end on Christmas Eve.

In the primitive church, the Christian year, like the Jewish year, began in the spring with the Pascha, and this ancient custom is continued in the Eastern church which still begins the year with Easter. But in the fourth century, when the festival of Christmas was introduced at Rome, it became the beginning of the church year, and the services in the oldest sacramentaries begin with the Vigil of Christmas.

The germ of Advent lies in a period of fasting and daily church attendance prescribed for those preparing for baptism on Epiphany (January 6). In the East, the Epiphany was a commemoration of both the birth and baptism of our Lord, and the festival was a natural time for the reception of candidates into the Christian fellowship. In the early centuries, the influence of the Eastern church was stronger in Spain and Gaul than that of the church in Rome. In Spain, in the fourth century, a three-week period of preparation began on December 17 and continued to January 6 with daily church attendance required. From Spain the custom spread to Gaul and thence to

northern Italy. However, in the meantime, Christmas, which
had been instituted at Rome in the fourth century, had spread
northward, and the period of preparation was prefixed to the
newer festival. It also became a general period of preparation
rather than one for baptismal candidates. During this period—
from the fourth to the seventh centuries—the length of Advent
varied from three to as many as seven weeks. In parts of Gaul,
it began on November 11 (St. Martin's Day) and was called
"St. Martin's Lent." In seventh-century England, the parallel
was drawn even more closely, and Advent had forty days. By
the end of the sixth century, Rome had set Advent at four
Sundays, though it was not until the time of Gregory VII, in
the eleventh century, that all deviations were finally suppressed.

With its acceptance as a four-Sunday season of preparation
for Christmas, Advent naturally became the beginning of the
church year. Remnants of the older and longer season still
remain in the propers appointed in both Lutheran and Anglican
churches for the Last Sunday after Trinity[1] and in the lessons
at the end of the Epiphany season.[2]

At first, Advent was not considered a penitential season—
certainly not to the same degree as Lent. As late as the twelfth
century, it was kept in some places with white altar colors. The
singing of alleluias continued during Advent, though the *Gloria
in excelsis* was eliminated from the Roman use in the eleventh
century. As time passed, Advent became more somber. The
color became violet as in Lent. Like Lent, it became a *tempora
clausa,* a period during which marriages were discouraged.[3]

[1] The Lutheran epistle, 2 Pet. 3:8-14, and gospel, Matt. 25:1-13 (The Ten
Virgins); the Anglican epistle, Jer. 23:5-8, all have an Advent note.
[2] The Fifth Sunday after the Epiphany is the parable of the wheat and the
tares (Matt. 13:24-30) in Lutheran, Anglican and Roman use. The last Sundays after Epiphany were "wandering Sundays" and were used to fill out the
Trinity season if needed. (See Epiphany, *infra.*)
[3] Adrian Fortescue, *The Ceremonies of the Roman Rite Described* (London:
Burns, Oates & Washbourne, 1943), p. 393: *Tempora clausa* "does not mean
marriage is forbidden, but only that there can be no nuptial mass and nuptial
blessing."

Today, in the Roman church, no flowers are permitted in
Advent except on Gaudete (the Third Sunday in Advent), and,
in the British Isles, there is a Wednesday and Friday fast as in
Lent. In the later Middle Ages, the penitential note was dominant. The famous medieval sequence *Dies irae,* written by
Thomas of Celano in the thirteenth century for the First Sunday in Advent, exhibits this spirit.[4]

Actually, Advent has come to have a threefold meaning for
the church: 1) the advent of our Lord in the flesh at Christmas;
2) the advent of the Lord in Word and in Spirit; and 3) the
advent of our Lord in glory at the end of time. If there is one
single note that runs through all of the meanings, it is that of
joyful anticipation. This is the spirit of the more ancient hymn
Veni Emmanuel (O come, O come, Emmanuel), which was
already venerable in the eighth century in its original form as
the "Great O's." These were antiphons sung before and after
the magnificat at vespers from December 17 to 23.[5] Each
begins with "O" and employs some Old Testament name and
prophetic type of the Messiah. Medieval calendars often carried
opposite December 17 the legend *O Sapientia* to mark the start
of the "Great O's." The hymn "O come, O come, Emmanuel"
is a cento of stanzas selected by John Mason Neale and put
in metrical form.

THE GREAT O's

Dec. 17—*O Sapientia:* O Wisdom proceeding from the
mouth of the Highest, reaching from eternity to eternity and
disposing all things with strength and sweetness: Come, teach
us the way of knowledge.

---

[4] Day of wrath! that day of mourning!
     See fulfilled the prophets' warning,
     Heaven and earth in ashes burning!, etc.
[5] An interesting coincidence that December 17 is also the date of the beginning of the first known Advent season in fourth-century Spain.

Dec. 18—*O Adonai:* O Lord and Leader of Israel, who didst appear to Moses in the burning bush and didst deliver the law to him on Sinai: Come redeem us by thine outstretched arm.

Dec. 19—*O Radix Jesse:* O Root of Jesse, who standest as an ensign of the people; before whom kings open not their mouths; to whom the nation shall pray: Come and deliver us, make no tarrying.

Dec. 20—*O Clavis David:* O Key of David and Sceptre of Israel, who openest and none shutteth, who shuttest and none openeth: Come and release from prison those who sit in darkness and in the shadow of death.

Dec. 21—*O Oriens:* O Dayspring, Splendor of eternal light and Sun of righteousness: Come and enlighten those that sit in darkness and in the shadow of death.

Dec. 22—*O Rex Gentium:* O King of Nations, their desire and the cornerstone that binds them in one: Come and save man whom thou formedst of clay.

Dec. 23—*O Emmanuel:* O Emmanuel, our King and Lawgiver, the Expectation and Saviour of the nations: Come and save us, O Lord our God.

THE ADVENT WREATH

The custom of having an "Advent Tree" or "Advent Wreath" in churches and sometimes in homes became popular in northern Europe, and has become increasingly popular in many places in the present day.

The Advent Tree is a small fir or spruce planted in a pot and decorated with a new light each day, or each Sunday, beginning with the First Sunday in Advent. With each new light, an Old Testament prophecy concerning the coming of Christ is read, printed on a card and placed on the tree beside the new light. Each time a new light is lighted, all those already there are lighted, too. Finally on Christmas Eve, the tree is aglow with lights.[6] The Advent Wreath is a wreath of spruce or fir hung in churches or in homes. On the First Sunday in Advent a red candle is fastened to the wreath and lighted. Each Sunday another candle is lighted; in homes a white candle is added each day, or sometimes paper stars with an Old Testament prophecy on one side and the New Testament fulfilment on the other.[7] The use of the Advent Wreath seems to have spread to England at one time, and medieval inventories of church ornaments list "rowells" which have baffled modern English churchmen. These rowells or trendles were hoops to which the candles were affixed.[8]

EMBER DAYS

The Wednesday, Friday and Saturday following December 13 (St. Lucy's Day) are "Ember Days" in the Roman and Anglican churches, with ordinations at St. Peter's in the Vatican on Saturday. The Ember Days were continued in many early Lutheran orders of the sixteenth century, but they were gradually replaced by other days of penance and by lectures on the catechism. Days of penance (*Busstage*) were proclaimed by rulers from time to time, but Lent and Advent, since they were already penitential seasons, were the favorite times for observing them.[9] The Wittenberg Order of 1533 replaced the Ember

[6] Georg Rietschel, *Weihnachten in Kirche, Kunst und Volksleben* (Bielefeld und Leipzig: Velhagen & Klasing, 1902), p. 154.

[7] Emmanuel Poppen in *Christmas* (Minneapolis: Augsburg, 1931), p. 16.

[8] J. T. Micklethwaite, *The Ornaments of the Rubric,* Alcuin Club, Tract I, 3rd ed. (London: Longmans, Green & Co., 1901), p. 46: "It seems to have belonged to Christmastide and to have been in use in many places. . . . The thing seems to have been a hoop with candles fixed to it which was hung up in the chancel or before the rood." In Reading in 1506 a holly bush was set up before the rood. The Christmas tree was not introduced into England until the nineteenth century.

[9] In Saxony, John George proclaimed one in 1633 during the Thirty Years' War; John George II another in 1664 after the war with the Turks. In Saxony and Saxe-Weimar one of the *Busstage* was in the first week in Advent, the other in the first week in Lent.

Days by preaching on the catechism during the first two weeks
of Advent and Lent and at two other times. There were two
sessions daily on Monday, Tuesday, Thursday and Friday of
each week.[10] Other Lutheran orders followed the same practice originally. Today Ember Days, days of penance and
lectures on the catechism, have all disappeared from the Lutheran calendar.

OTHER CUSTOMS

In Italy the last days of Advent are marked by the entry into
Rome of the *pifferare* from Calabria, who play bagpipes at the
shrines of the Virgin Mary just as they think the shepherds did
at the birth of Christ. In England, poor women carry Advent
images, representing our Lord and Mary, from house to house
as they beg. In Sweden, St. Lucy's Day (December 13) is a
time of folk gaiety and festivity.

In recent times in America the proper observance of Advent
has suffered greatly from the commercialization of Christmas.
To stimulate sales of Christmas gifts, stores and communities
often use Christmas decorations as early as November 1. Christmas carols and music are heard so continously that Advent is
all but completely blanketed and Christmas is spoiled long
before it arrives. Even the church has been guilty of abetting
this secular attitude. Christmas is often observed on what is
popularly called "Christmas Sunday" which is actually the
Fourth Sunday in Advent, rather than on Christmas Day.[11]
Choirs often present their programs of Christmas music before
Christmas and during the Advent season. In the face of such
heavy opposition, it is difficult to combat the popular feeling
that Christmas is over on Christmas Day. Actually, for the
church down through the centuries, Christmas begins on

[10] This happened also in Sweden. Cf. Gustaf Lindberg, *Kyrkans Heliga Ar*
(Stockholm: Svenska Kyrkans Diakonistyrelses Bokförlag, 1937), p. 372.
[11] Cf. Seidenspinner, *op. cit.*

Christmas Eve and continues everywhere until Epiphany, and in some places until Candlemas (February 2). The exchanging of gifts on Christmas is not universal and some countries have not suffered from commercialism as much as America has. Whatever can be done to preserve the integrity and spirit of Advent should be done. Christmas should be observed in the church on Christmas Eve and Christmas Day. Christmas music and carols should begin then and be sung throughout the Christmas season. No one would think of singing an Easter hymn during Lent or Holy Week!

THE FIRST SUNDAY IN ADVENT
(ADVENT SUNDAY)

The First Sunday in Advent, often called Advent Sunday, is the church's new year's day, and is the Sunday falling nearest to, or upon, St. Andrew's Day, November 30. It may occur between November 27 and December 3. The propers are all anticipatory, looking toward the coming of Christ. The introit is the same in Lutheran as the Roman use, as is the gradual. Psalm 25:4 appears in both of them. The collect is the first of three "stir up" collects assigned to Advent. It comes from the Gregorian Sacramentary, and is the same as the Roman use. The Anglicans use a collect written in 1549 for the First Prayer Book of Edward VI, which, since 1662, is repeated every day in Advent.

The epistle from Romans has always been difficult because of its beginning in English, "And that, knowing the time. . . ." It is much clearer with a liturgical introduction such as has been used in the Christian church for centuries, "Brethren, ye know the time. . . ." The epistle is the same in Lutheran and Roman use. The Anglicans begin with verse 8, but Rom. 13:8-10 is the epistle used by both Lutherans and Roman Catholics for the Fourth Sunday after the Epiphany.

The gospel, which should be understood symbolically, re-counts the entry of our Lord into Jerusalem on Palm Sunday. In Lutheran use, it is the only gospel which is repeated during the year. It comes from the earliest lectionaries of the Western church in the seventh century, but the modern Roman Missal has displaced it by Luke 21:25-33, a shorter version of the gospel in Lutheran use for the Second Sunday in Advent (Luke 21:25-36). At the Reformation, the Anglicans added verses 10-13. The new Lutheran *Service Book* permits the use of Luke 3:1-6 (the call of John the Baptist) as an alternate gospel. However, the use of the triumphal entry is traditional on this Sunday rather than on Palm Sunday when the traditional gospel was either the entire passion according to St. Matthew or the story of the anointing at Bethany.

> *Propers:* Introit—Ps. 25:1-3a, 4[12]
> Collect—Gregorian
> Lesson—Jer. 31:31-34
> Epistle—Rom. 13:11-14
> Gradual—Pss. 25:3-4; 85:7
> Gospel—Matt. 21:1-9 or Luke 3:1-6
> Creed—Nicene[13]
> Proper Preface—Advent
> Color—Violet

THE SECOND SUNDAY IN ADVENT

As the thought of the First Sunday in Advent was the entry of Christ into Jerusalem, so the thought of the Second Sunday is that of his second coming in triumph at the end of time.

---

[12] The letters "a" or "b" after a verse number indicate respectively the first or second half of the verse.

[13] The Lutheran rubric provides that "the Nicene Creed shall be used on all Festivals and whenever there is a Communion." *Common Service Book,* text edition, p. 485. The Sundays in Advent are all festivals. *Ibid.,* p. 491.

The gospel is the ancient one and is in both Lutheran and Anglican use. The modern Missal has transferred the gospel for the Third Sunday in Advent to this Sunday.

The epistle, which is the same in all three churches, is part of St. Paul's admonition to both Jewish and Gentile Christians to settle their differences by the study of the Scriptures which would convince them that both Jew and Gentile are one in Christ.

Both epistle and gospel lend themselves to the observance of Universal Bible Sunday which, set for the second Sunday in December, often falls on the Second Sunday in Advent.[14] This Sunday also has another and more ancient connotation. Occasionally the ancient Roman stational church (in which the bishop celebrated mass on a specified day) has left some mark on the day's propers. This Sunday is such an instance. The stational church was the Church of the Holy Cross in Jerusalem, which had formerly been the Sessorian Palace and the home of Helen, mother of the Emperor Constantine. Here she enshrined a relic of the "true cross" and converted the palace into a basilica. Both the introit (Daughter of Zion, behold thy salvation cometh) and the gradual (Our feet shall stand within thy gates, O Jerusalem) are believed to reflect their original use in this ancient Roman stational church of the fourth century.

> *Propers:* Introit—Isa. 62:11; 30:30, 29; Ps. 80:1
> Collect—Gelasian
> Lesson—Mal. 4:1-6
> Epistle—Rom. 15:4-13
> Gradual—Pss. 50:2-3a, 5; 122:1-2
> Gospel—Luke 21:25-33

[14] Epistle: "Whatsoever things were written aforetime were written for our learning." Gospel: "Heaven and earth shall pass away: but my words shall not pass away."

Creed—Nicene
Proper Preface—Advent
Color—Violet

THE THIRD SUNDAY IN ADVENT

The figure of St. John the Baptist is introduced in the gospel for this Sunday as the forerunner of Christ, and the epistle continues last Sunday's note of the second coming in its admonition to "judge nothing before the time, until the Lord come, who both will bring to light the hidden things of darkness, and will make manifest the counsels of the hearts." Its references also to the "ministers of Christ" and the "stewards of the mysteries of God" carry us back to the time when this Sunday, coming at the time of the December Ember Days, was associated with ordinations. In the present Missal this epistle has been moved to the Fourth Sunday in Advent to make it immediately follow the ordinations. Ancient usage, still followed in Lutheran and Anglican churches, appoints it for this Sunday.

The introit, collect and gradual are the same in Lutheran and Roman use; the Anglicans have a collect prepared in 1662. The gospel is the same in Lutheran and Anglican use; in Roman use the gospel for the Fourth Sunday has been moved to the Third Sunday. In the Roman Catholic church this Sunday breaks Advent just as Laetare breaks Lent. It is known as Gaudete Sunday from the first word of the introit. Rose instead of violet is permitted as the color of the day; flowers are allowed on altars. But, for evangelical Christians, there must always be a note of joy in a season which anticipates, as Advent does, the coming of the Saviour.

Propers: Introit—Phil. 4:4-6; Ps. 85:1
Collect—Gelasian
Lesson—Isa. 40:1-8

Epistle—I Cor. 4:1-5
Gradual—Ps. 80:1b, 2b, 1a, 2b
Gospel—Matt. 11:2-10
Creed—Nicene
Proper Preface—Advent
Color—Violet

THE FOURTH SUNDAY IN ADVENT

The Fourth and last Sunday in Advent has been an "orphan" for centuries so far as its true nature is concerned. In contemporary America it is often called "Christmas Sunday"—an intrusion from nonliturgical Protestantism of Puritan background which, having divorced all religious observances from Christmas, sought to salve its conscience by transferring these observances to the previous Sunday. As a result, in many Protestant churches this Sunday is pre-empted by Christmas "messages," Christmas decorations and Christmas music, thus losing its own status as the culminating Sunday in the season of anticipation. Even liturgical churches have been hard put to keep Christmas out of the last Sunday in Advent.

In the ancient church, it was not the anticipation of Christmas that overshadowed this Sunday, but the ordinations held on the previous Saturday. As a result, it is probable that the propers originally appointed for this day were transferred to the Ember Days (Wednesday, Friday and Saturday) which preceded it. The present introit and gradual are the same as the Wednesday Ember Day; the gospel, the same as for the Ember Saturday.

The introit and gradual are the same in Roman and Lutheran use, as is the collect, which has been expanded and edited in Anglican use. The epistle is the same in both Lutheran and Anglican use, but the Missal transfers it forward to the Third Sunday in Advent, and transposes the epistle for the Third

Sunday to the Fourth. In the gospel for the Third Sunday we hear our Lord's testimony to John the Baptist; today we hear John's testimony to Jesus. The Roman gospel is Luke 3:1-6, which is relatively new and which is, in Lutheran use, given as the alternate gospel for the First Sunday in Advent.

> *Propers:* Introit—Isa. 45:8a; Ps. 19:1
> Collect—Gelasian
> Lesson—Deut. 18:15-19 or Isa. 40:9-11
> Epistle—Phil. 4:4-7
> Gradual—Pss. 145:18, 21; 40:17b
> Gospel—John 1:19-28
> Creed—Nicene
> Proper Preface—Advent
> Color—Violet

7.

CHRISTMAS AND ITS SEASON

The exact time of the birth of Jesus—the day, the month and even the year—is not known. Errors in the calendar now place the year of his birth in 4 B.C. (Before Christ). It is, however, probable that he was born in the late fall or winter. Mary and Joseph had to return to their home town to be enumerated in the census ordered by Caesar Augustus. It is highly unlikely that such a census would have been ordered in an agricultural country until after all the crops were in and the fall planting had been completed.

But for several centuries no one cared much about the date of our Lord's birth anyway. For one thing, his life and work, and especially his resurrection, were so much more important to the early Christians than the details of his earthly life that scarcely any attention was paid the latter. For another, the early church was impressed with the imminence of his return and the commemoration of his birth seemed unimportant. And finally, it was the date of the death of a Christian—his birth to eternity and his entrance into the joy of his Lord—which was of greater significance than the date of his birth in time. The date of our Lord's death on Good Friday was observed as part of the Pascha, and the days which followed, from Easter to Pentecost, formed one uninterrupted season of thanksgiving and rejoicing for his triumph over sin and death and for the unending presence of the Holy Spirit.

In the earliest centuries, there was one festival which com-

memorated both the birth and baptism of Christ, Epiphany
(January 6). The date of December 25 was instituted at
Rome before 336. The choice of the date was determined by
an already existing pagan festival there, the birth of the sun-
god, *Natalis solis invicti.* In the fourth century the winter
solstice occurred on December 25, instead of December 21, as
at present. It was the shortest day of the year, and from then
on the sun returned for a longer period each day. The "uncon-
querable sun" was "reborn." The Emperor Constantine had
been brought up in this religious cult, and it was quite natural
that the Christians should see in it a striking analogy to Jesus,
the Sun of Righteousness. The suggestion that this may have
been a quite conscious connection from the very beginning
lingers on in the ancient collect for the early service on Christmas, "O God, who hast made this most holy night to shine with
the brightness of the true Light: Grant, we beseech thee, that
as we have known on earth the mysteries of that Light, we
may also come to the fullness of his joy in heaven."

From Rome the festival spread slowly, partly because of the
celebration already existing in the East, Spain and Gaul, on
January 6. Christmas was observed in Antioch about 375; in
Alexandria in the fifth century. Gradually it had a catalytic
effect on the Epiphany, removing from it the birth of Christ.
This was expedited by the Christological controversies and the
struggle against Arianism that raged in the church in the fourth
century. The divinity of Christ was questioned, and a festival
which commemorated the Incarnation alone was welcomed by
orthodox Christians.

Not only theologically, but also liturgically, the new festival
was important. There were a number of festivals dependent
upon its date. By a very simple logic, since Jesus was supposed
to have lived a perfect number of years, the date of the annunciation and of his crucifixion became March 25. His circum-

cision, eight days after his birth, fell on January 1; the presentation in the Temple (later known as the Purification of the Virgin Mary, or Candlemas) was forty days later on February 2; the nativity of John the Baptist, who was six months older than Jesus, was June 24. In the East, when January 6 was observed as Jesus' birthday, the annunciation and crucifixion had been on April 6; the presentation on February 14, etc.

As early as 400, games in the Roman circus were banned on Christmas along with Easter and Epiphany and gradually, as with the other major festivals of the church year, the celebration of Christmas was extended over a longer period—in the case of Christmas, two or three days. This tradition was especially strong in Germany. Muhlenberg in 1742, his first year in America, observed Christmas, Second Christmas Day and Third Christmas Day.[1]

In England, the period of general festivity extended from Christmas to Epiphany, which was known popularly as Twelfth Night. The name "Christmas" itself is an old English title. "Christ's Mass," just as Candlemas and Michaelmas were similar popular contractions. In other places, Christmastide extended from Christmas Eve to Candlemas; in some to the octave of the Epiphany (January 13); in others to Candlemas or to Septuagesima, whichever came first.

There have been many reactions against these customs. The Puritans reacted violently against Christmas during Cromwell's rule in seventeenth-century England. From 1644 to 1660 its observance was illegal; church services were forbidden and the churches had to remain closed. Work was to continue as usual. Yuletide was known as Fooltide. In Scotland, the observance of Christmas was regarded as the mark of popery. While the law was repealed under Charles II, the nonconformists continued to keep watch, and a deep suspicion of

[1] Tappert & Doberstein, *op. cit.,* vol. I, pp. 73-74.

Christmas has continued to linger among their spiritual descendants in both the Old and New Worlds. In Massachusetts
in 1639, a law provided that "whoever shall be found observing any such day as Christmas or the like, either by forbearing
of labour, fasting, or in any other way, shall be fined five
shillings." In contemporary America, Christmas is a favorite
target for Jehovah's Witnesses[2] who hold that "the Christian
would not be justified in having anything to do with it (Christmas) because of its pagan origins. Both Jews and Christians
were warned not to have anything to do with pagan religions,
and the early church all [sic] understood it that way."

It is certainly true that many of the folk customs which
have come to be associated with Christmas are of non-Christian
origin. It is also true that, if they obscure the true meaning of
the festival, they should not be continued. But it is also true
that many of the associations are helpful in emphasizing the
real significance of Christmas—the coming of God in human
form in the birth of Jesus in Bethlehem. The créche, for
instance, dates back to St. Francis of Assisi who is said to have
built the first one in 1223. The Christmas carols are among
the best-loved items in all Christian music, sung by Christians
and non-Christians alike. The nativity plays, which had their
origin in the reading of the gospel story by priests, choir boys
and cantors, have added much to the religious meaning of the
season.

Clustered about Christmas Day are several important minor
festivals: St. Stephen, Martyr (December 26); St. John,
Apostle, Evangelist (December 27); Holy Innocents (December 28). The octave of Christmas became the Circumcision
(January 1). In many Lutheran orders the first two of these
festivals were replaced by Second and Third Christmas Days,
and the Circumcision by New Year's Day—a civil holiday. In

[2] "Why Celebrate Christmas?" *Awake,* December 22, 1952, pp. 21-24.

recent years, however, in both Europe and America, Lutheran orders have restored the ancient and historic observances of liturgical Christianity.

CHRISTMAS DAY

At first (to the fifth century), there was only one mass at Rome on Christmas Day. Today there are three—the first commemorating the eternal generation of the Son from the Father, the second his Incarnation and birth in the world, and the third his birth through grace in our hearts. The first is at midnight in the Church of St. Mary Major where Constantine's mother, Helen, enshrined an alleged fragment of the manger in which Jesus was born. The second, called the "Aurora Mass," is held at dawn in the Church of St. Anastasia. It contains a commemoration of St. Anastasia of Sirmium in a collect, secret and postcommunion. Both the stational church for this service and the commemoration have led scholars to believe that, prior to the fourth century, December 25 was St. Anastasia's day in the calendar. The third mass is held on Christmas morning in the Church of St. Mary Major.

Of these three services, the Lutheran and Anglican reformers retained the first and third, though the propers for the former disappeared from Anglican use in the Second Prayer Book of Edward VI in 1552. American Episcopalians restored them in 1892, and the Irish and Scottish Anglicans followed suit in 1927 and 1929, respectively. In Lutheran use, the propers for the Aurora Mass were used on Second Christmas Day, but in the new *Service Book,* which provides propers for St. Stephen's Day on December 26, the gospel from the Aurora Mass becomes the lesson for vespers on Christmas Day, and the Aurora Mass epistle is assigned to the Second Sunday after Christmas.[3]

---

[3] Luke 2:15-20 and Titus 3:4-7, respectively. The Second Sunday after Christmas occurs only in years in which Christmas falls on Wednesday, Thursday, Friday or Saturday.

The First Service

All of the propers are the same as those in Roman use and
are of ancient provenance. The epistle from Titus 2 combines
the thought of the first and second advents of our Lord. The
gospel from Luke 2 is the narrative of the nativity and particularly timely for midnight services. Its words form a classic
of English prose and are probably known by heart by more
people than any other portion of the New Testament of comparable length. It is the inspiration of the great liturgical hymn
sung every Sunday at the beginning of the liturgy,[4] the *Gloria
in excelsis Deo.* The collect is the ancient Gelasian collect including the reference to Christ as "the true light" with its
reminiscence of the Roman pagan festival of the *Natalis solis
invicti* which Christmas replaced.

> *Propers:* Introit—Pss. 2:7; 93:1
> Collect—Gelasian
> Lesson—Isa. 9:2-7
> Epistle—Titus 2:11-14 or I John 4:7-16
> Gradual—Pss. 110:3, 1; 2:7
> Gospel—Luke 2:1-14
> Creed—Nicene
> Proper Preface—Christmas
> Color—White

The Later Service

The later service on Christmas Day is less narrative and
more theological. The propers are all those of the traditional
third mass of the day, and the lessons convey the theological
implications of the Incarnation: the revelation of God in time
in the person of his Son, Jesus Christ. The gospel, John

---

[4] The liturgy reviews the life of Christ, from his Nativity (*Gloria in excelsis*)
to his Pascha (Holy Communion).

1:1-14, is the so-called "last gospel" which is read at the conclusion of the mass in the Roman Catholic church on virtually every occasion. At the time that this gospel was appointed for Christmas Day, Christmas was the beginning of the church year. It is worthy of passing notice that it is the gospel for Easter Day in the Eastern church which begins its church year with Easter. "The force of this circumstance was all the more impressive by virtue of the opening words of the gospel, 'In the beginning.' " [5]

> *Propers:* Introit—Isa. 9:6; Ps. 98:1
> Collect—Gelasian
> Lesson—Isa. 45:1-8
> Epistle—Heb. 1:1-12
> Gradual—Pss. 98:3b, 4a, 2; 95:1a, 6a
> Gospel—John 1:1-14
> Creed—Nicene
> Proper Preface—Christmas
> Color—White

ST. STEPHEN, PROTOMARTYR
DECEMBER 26

From about the fifth or sixth centuries, the Western church has immediately followed Christmas with three festivals of "martyrs": St. Stephen, martyr in will and in deed; St. John, martyr in will but not in deed; of the Holy Innocents, martyrs in deed but not in will.

First to die for the faith was one whom St. Paul calls "thy martyr Stephen." [6] The account of his martyrdom is in Acts 6:1—8:2. Stephen was one of the original seven deacons chosen by the twelve to supervise the work of the Christian

---

[5] Massey H. Shepherd, *The Oxford American Prayer Book Commentary* (New York: Oxford University Press, 1950), p. 97.
[6] Acts 22:20.

community in Jerusalem. His zeal and enthusiasm quickly brought him into conflict with the authorities. He was tried, convicted and stoned to death with the consent, among others, of Saul. Modern psychologists trace the subsequent feverish, anti-Christian activity and the consequent spectacular conversion of Saul into St. Paul to its beginnings in the trial and death of St. Stephen.

It is quite possible that St. Stephen may have been remembered on the day of his martyrdom from the actual event. At least his name appears in the earliest lists of martyrs known and in almost every Christian calendar of whatever date. When Christianity became legal in the fourth century, his day was already established in Jerusalem, and in the fifth century Pope Simplicius (468-483) built and dedicated a church of St. Stephen on the Coelian Hill in Rome. This basilica, called San Stefano Rotundo because of its circular design, became the stational church for the mass on December 26.

The introit is historic in the Western church. The collect has been edited over the centuries and in its present expanded form comes from the English Prayer Book of 1662.[7] The original Latin was a simple prayer that we might be given grace to imitate him whose martyrdom we celebrate in praying for our enemies and persecutors. The epistle for the day was originally Acts 6:8—7:60—one of the longest lections of the year and including the entire speech of St. Stephen. In the Missal it has been shortened to Acts 6:8-10 and 7:54-60.[8] In Anglican use it has been reduced to Acts 7:55-60. Lutheran use permits either the ancient long lesson, or the modern Roman use. The gospel is traditional and is in all uses.

[7] Massey H. Shepherd, op. cit., p. 99: "The 1662 revisers expanded this Collect into the form we now have, filling in material from the Epistle, and changing the address from the first to the second Person of the Godhead. The result is not altogether felicitous."

[8] This is one of the very few places the church allows a mosaic lesson. The general principle is that all lessons should be continuous. In this case the use of Acts 6:8-10 is essential since it provides the setting.

Propers: Introit—Ps. 119:23a, 95a, 22b, 1
        Collect—*Book of Common Prayer,* 1662
        Lesson—2 Chronicles 24:17-22
        Epistle—Acts 6:8—7:60 or Acts 7:54-60
        Gradual—Matt. 5:10; Rev. 2:10b;
            Acts 7:56[9]
        Gospel—Matt. 23:34-39
        Creed—Nicene
        Proper Preface—All Saints
        Color—Red

<h2 style="text-align:center">ST. JOHN, APOSTLE, EVANGELIST
DECEMBER 27</h2>

The apostle commemorated on December 27 was, along with James and Peter, one of the "inner circle" of the twelve. Tradition associates him with the "disciple whom Jesus loved" and with the authorship of the Fourth Gospel, two epistles which bear his name, and the Book of Revelation. Modern biblical scholarship has raised serious questions about these traditions, but generally concedes that, even if the Apostle John did not actually write the books, they may rest upon his work. They are certainly part of the "Johannine tradition." John was the son of Zebedee and, with his brother James, was a partner in a fishing business on the shores of the Sea of Galilee when called by our Lord to become a disciple. Of all the twelve, he is the only one who is supposed to have met a natural, and not a martyr's death. After a period of exile at an advanced age on the Aegean island of Patmos, he is said to have died and been buried at Ephesus. In the fourth century his alleged grave was opened for the purpose of transferring his remains to a new church being erected in his honor in Con-

---

[9] Only the last verse of the Lutheran gradual is historic. In ancient use the first two verses were the same as the introit for the day, from Psalm 119.

stantinople. Only powder was found, giving rise to a tradition
that John had been taken up to heaven bodily. In some early
calendars his day is called "The departure of St. John," or "The
assumption of St. John, Evangelist."

The oldest calendars in the East combine both John and
James on December 27, as early as the fourth century. By the
sixth century, however, when the festival was accepted at Rome,
St. John appears alone. In Lutheran orders of the sixteenth
century, St. John's Day was retained in some places, but abro-
gated in others in favor of Third Christmas Day.

In Christian iconography St. John is represented by an eagle,
expressing the soaring sublimity of the writings ascribed to
him; or with a cup and serpent, or palm branch and scroll;
sometimes as an old man in vestments being lifted out of his
grave at the foot of an altar.

In the Middle Ages wine was blessed on St. John's Day in
many churches in northern Europe and England. This wine
was then given to brides and grooms at the end of wedding
ceremonies during the ensuing year. In St. Lawrence's Church,
Reading, England, there was a silver chalice, given the church
in 1534 " 'to be carried before all brydds that were wedded in
St. Laurence's Church.' The ceremonial drinking together in
church at the end of the wedding service was a recognized
custom, and the cup was formally blessed by the priest." [10] A
similar custom prevailed in Saxony and elsewhere in Germany.[11] The cup was known as the Love of St. John, *St.
Johannis Liebe* or *Amor St. Iohannus.* So prevalent was the
practice that the sixteenth century Lutheran Pfalz-Neuberg

[10] J. T. Micklethwaite, *The Ornaments of the Rubric, op. cit.,* p. 51. "The
note in the Reading parish books shows that the cup was carried into the church
in the bride's procession."

[11] Martin Gebert, *Vetus Liturgia Alemannica,* 1776. Part III, Disquisitio IX—
De Festis. "Er hat S. Iohannis Liebe zu einem Zeichen wahrer Liebe ihnen zu
trinken geben." The ceremony on St. John's Day was called "Iohannis-Weyhe,"
i.e., St. John's Blessing. "Vocatur etiam hoc festum apud nos Iohannis-Weyhe."

church order specifically forbids the consecration of wine on St. John's Day.

The propers are traditional except for the epistle which was Ecclus. 15:1-6. The reformers, both Lutheran and Anglican, discarded lessons from the Old Testament Apocrypha though the Apocrypha remained in Lutheran bibles. Instead, an epistle from 1 John 1 was substituted. The gospel is the same in Lutheran and Roman use; the Anglicans have added one additional verse. The collect belongs to the oldest sacramentary, the Leonine, though it was shortened in the Gregorian.[12]

> *Propers:* Introit—Common of Apostles
> Collect—Leonine
> Lesson—Hos. 14:1-9 or Hos. 11:1-4
> Epistle—1 John 1:1-10
> Gradual—Common of Apostles
> Gospel—John 21:19b-24
> Creed—Nicene
> Proper Preface—All Saints
> Color—White

THE HOLY INNOCENTS, MARTYRS
DECEMBER 28

This day, December 28, is the commemoration of the unknown (both in name and number) children of Bethlehem slaughtered by King Herod in his futile attempt to kill the infant Jesus "born king of the Jews."[13] The church early acknowledged them as unwitting martyrs for Christ and their day appears in calendars in North Africa in the fifth century.

---

[12] Literally: "Mercifully enlighten thy Church, O Lord, that, illuminated by the teachings of thy blessed Apostle and Evangelist, John, it may come to its eternal reward." The English phrase "may so walk in the light of thy truth" was added in the 1662 Prayer Book and adopted by Lutherans from that source.
[13] Matt. 2:16-18.

By the end of that century, the observance had spread throughout Western Christianity, and from the sixth century it appears in every calendar.[14]

In the early Middle Ages, this day was the occasion of the Feast of Fools or *Narrenfest*. A boy bishop was elected and the mass was parodied. Foul-smelling incense was used and there was a general roughhouse in the churches. In 1198 the papal legate protested against this sort of thing in Notre Dame, the Cathedral of Paris, in a letter to Bishop Odo. In 1473 the Synod of Toledo banned such performances. The date varied in different places—Christmas, St. Stephen's, St. John's, Holy Innocents', or New Year's Day—but the most usual days were Holy Innocents or St. Stephen.[15]

In many Lutheran church orders the day was dropped, not for theological reasons, but because of the three-day Christmas observance which preceded it. The gospel was retained, however, and in some orders was assigned to the Sunday after Christmas; in recent American books to the Second Sunday after Christmas. In any case, of course, it appears out of sequence in the church year, since it is a direct consequence of the visit of the Wise Men which the Western church associates with the Epiphany (January 6). The ancient Mozarabic church (Spanish) placed it after Epiphany, just as it also placed the Annunciation, with more consistency, in Advent.

The propers are traditional and the lessons are the same in Lutheran, Roman and Anglican use. The collect is Gelasian. In the modern Roman Catholic church the *Gloria in excelsis* is omitted on this day.

[14] There may have been an earlier celebration in the East. McArthur, *op. cit.*, p. 155, thinks that the occasion mentioned by Etheria at Bethlehem forty days after Easter was Holy Innocents. This was in the fourth century.

[15] Heinrich Alt, *Das Kirchenjahr* (Berlin: G. W. F. Müller, 1860), p. 316ff.: "Offas pingues supra cornu altaris, ludum taxillorum exarabant, thurificabant de fumo foetido, ex corio veterum sotularium, et per totam Ecclesiam currebant et saltabant."

Propers: Introit—Ps. 8:2a, 1a
            Collect—Gelasian
            Lesson—Jer. 31:15-17
            Epistle—Rev. 14:1-5
            Gradual—Pss. 124:7, 8; 113:1b
            Gospel—Matt. 2:13-18
            Creed—Nicene
            Proper Preface—All Saints
            Color—Red

THE FIRST SUNDAY AFTER CHRISTMAS

The propers for this Sunday are those of the pre-Reformation use for the Sunday within the octave of Christmas. Most of the other days within the octave already had their own propers—St. Stephen (December 26), St. John (December 27), Holy Innocents (December 28), St. Thomas of Canterbury (December 29), and St. Sylvester (December 31). Since the octave itself was the Circumcision, the only day on which these propers would be used would be on December 30 if that day were a Sunday. In Lutheran use, the only open days would be December 29, 30 and 31, although the last of these was continued in some European Lutheran calendars after the Reformation, and is still observed to some extent—if not as St. Sylvester's Day, at least as *Todtenfest,* a memorial service for the faithful departed.

The collect is Gelasian and used in both Lutheran and Roman rites. The Anglicans use a 1549 collect prepared for Christmas Day and repeated on this Sunday. The Gospel, Luke 2:33-40, is chronologically out of place since it immediately follows that for the Presentation of our Lord (February 2). Cranmer did no better in the *Book of Common Prayer* when he replaced this lesson with Matt. 1:18-21 which is the account of the annunciation.

Propers: Introit—Ps. 93:5, 2, 1a
         Collect—Gelasian
         Lesson—Isa. 63:7-16
         Epistle—Gal. 4:1-7
         Gradual—Pss. 45:2a, 1; 93:1a
         Gospel—Luke 2:33-40
         Creed—Nicene or Apostles'
         Proper Preface—Christmas
         Color—White

THE CIRCUMCISION AND THE NAME OF JESUS
(NEW YEAR'S DAY)

Originally, and in all the ancient service books, January 1 was the octave of Christmas, *Octava Domini.* Then as now, however, the day was a popular holiday marked by dancing, masquerades and general pagan gaiety. Councils of the church in France, Spain and Italy found it necessary from the fifth century to forbid the participation of the faithful in these celebrations; to order them instead to attend church; and finally to set the day as one of fasting, litanies and penance. In 650 it became a day of holy obligation on which everyone had to attend church.

The association of the day with the circumcision of Jesus depended on Luke 2:21 when, in obedience to the levitical law, the infant Jesus was taken to the temple on the eighth day for his naming and the fulfilment of ritual ceremonies. This association in the calendar appears to have been made first in Gaul. In the ninth century, Roman calendars abandoned the title, *Octava Domini,* in favor of *Circumcisio Domini.*

Until the sixteenth century, both the Circumcision and the Name of Jesus were jointly commemorated on January 1, and the title in many Lutheran orders is The Circumcision and the Name of Jesus. In 1530, after the Reformation, Pope Clement

VII granted the Franciscans permission to celebrate the Feast of the Holy Name as a separate festival, and in 1721 Innocent XIII extended the observance to the whole Roman Catholic church and set the time as the Second Sunday after the Epiphany. This festival is the special concern of the Holy Name Society today.

The liturgy of the church makes no reference to the beginning of the civil year on January 1. "Watch night" services are of nonliturgical origin, and represent a latter-day attempt of the church to temper the excesses of New Year's Eve, just as the Feast of the Circumcision once attempted the same thing for New Year's Day.

The propers for the day are somewhat confused historically. The present Missal repeats the introit for the third mass of Christmas and the epistle for the second mass of Christmas. The collect is more concerned with the Virgin Mary than with Christ. The Anglican collect is a 1549 composition of Cranmer, based on an ancient Gregorian collect. The Lutheran collect is from the Gregorian, but in its translation a curious printer's error in the Anglican collect was copied. The 1552 Anglican revisers wrote "grant us the true circumcision of the spirit" and the printers capitalized Spirit![16] Rather than repeat the Christmas epistle, Lutherans use Gal. 3:23-29. The Anglicans have been unable to agree on a suitable one.[17] The gradual is the same in Lutheran and Roman use, as is the gospel, the shortest in the church year: Luke 2:21. In Anglican use, the gospel is Luke 2:15-21, including the continuation of the Christmas gospel with the visit of the shepherds to the manger.

[16] Massey H. Shepherd, op. cit., p. 106, "The eminent liturgical scholar, Dr. F. E. Brightman, considered that the Collect and Epistle (Rom. 4:8-14) adopted in the 1549 Book had 'altered the proportion of things, and in fact had turned the day into a commemoration of circumcision, rather than of the Circumcision of our Lord, not to edification.'"

[17] England: Rom. 4:8-14; America: Phil. 2:9-13; Scotland and Ireland: Eph. 2:11-18.

    Propers: Introit—Ps. 8:1, 4; Isa. 63:16b
             Collect—Gregorian
             Lesson—Josh. 24:14-24
             Epistle—Gal. 3:23-29
             Gradual—Ps. 98:3b, 4b, 2; Heb. 1:1, 2a
             Gospel—Luke 2:21
             Creed—Nicene
             Proper Preface—Christmas
             Color—White

THE SECOND SUNDAY AFTER CHRISTMAS

This Sunday was a "vacant" day in the old service books, with no appointed propers. They were not needed, since the only days upon which it could fall were already provided with propers. January 2 is the octave of St. Stephen; January 3, of St. John; January 4, of Holy Innocents; and January 5 is the Vigil of the Epiphany. In Lutheran use the introit, collect, and gradual for the First Sunday after Christmas are repeated. The epistle, Titus 3:4-7, formerly read on Second Christmas Day, is appointed. The gospel is the continuation of the gospel for the later service on Christmas Day, in which all Anglican books except the American (Matt. 2:19-23) agree.

    Propers: Introit—Same as the First Sunday after
               Christmas
             Collect—Gelasian
             Lesson—1 Sam. 2:1-10
             Epistle—Titus 3:4-7
             Gradual—Same as the First Sunday after
               Christmas
             Gospel—John 1:14-18
             Creed—Nicene or Apostles'
             Proper Preface—Christmas
             Color—White

8.

THE EPIPHANY AND
ITS SEASON

Next to the season from Easter to Pentecost, the Epiphany is the oldest of the festivals of the church year. Recent scholarship finds evidence of its existence in the second century in Asia Minor and Egypt, where January 6 was observed as a commemoration of both the birth and the baptism of Jesus.[1] Like Christmas, which developed later at Rome, the Epiphany took its date from a pagan festival which it replaced; and like Christmas, it, too, was a solstice festival. In 1996 B.C., during the reign of Amenemhet I of Thebes, the winter solstice occurred on January 6, and a night festival on January 5-6 celebrated the birth of Aeon from Kore, the Virgin.[2] In the course of time, and because of the error in measuring time, the solstice ceased to occur on January 6, but the festival continued. When Alexandria was founded in 331 B.C., the solstice was December 25, and a new and "modern" pagan festival was instituted, known as Kikellia in Alexandria, and Kronia in Egypt. These festivals were the counterpart of the Roman solstice festival of the *Natalis solis invicti*. This made it easier for Christmas to be adopted in the east after the fourth century.

The word "epiphany" means manifestation, and the root of the word was often used to describe the dawn, and the appear-

[1] A. Alan McArthur, *op. cit.,* p. 31ff.
[2] Dom Bernard Botte, *Les Origines de la Noël et de l'Epiphanie* (Louvain, 1932).

ance of gods bringing help to men. The Epiphany was also called the Theophany, the Feast of the Manifestation, the Feast of Lights, the Feast of the Appearing of Christ. The earliest manifestations commemorated on the Epiphany were the birth and baptism of Jesus. From its solstice date there developed an association with the rebirth of light, an echo of which still persists in the lesson for the festival.[3] A further early association was with the changing of the water into wine at Cana, our Lord's first miracle and the subject of the traditional gospel for the Second Sunday after the Epiphany. This was probably consciously designed to sublimate the pagan festival of the wine-god Dionysus on January 5-6 which was popular in many parts of the Near East.

It was only after the adoption of December 25 as the date of Christmas that the Epiphany was restricted in the East to the celebration of the baptism of our Lord. The Western church, on the other hand, with the exception of parts of Gaul and Spain which were under Eastern influence, seems to have associated with Epiphany not our Lord's baptism, but rather the visit of the Wise Men to Bethlehem. The reason for this association is obscure, but it may have been due to the transfer in the fourth century of the alleged relics of the Magi from Constantinople to Milan.

The visit of the Magi (Matt. 2:10ff.) took place some time after the birth of our Lord. When they reached Bethlehem, Joseph and Mary and the Infant Jesus were no longer in the stable, but in a house. Later, when Herod slaughtered the children in Bethlehem, hoping to eliminate Jesus among them, he set the upper age limit at two years. It is probable, therefore, that the visit of the Magi took place more than a year after the birth of Jesus. Even so conscienceless a ruler as Herod would hardly have made the age limit unnecessarily high. In addition,

---

[3] Isa. 60:1-6: "Arise, shine; for thy light is come. . . ."

our Lord was brought to the Temple at the age of eight days and again at forty days. Both of these events—the circumcision and the presentation—must have occurred before the flight into Egypt and subsequent return to Nazareth. This is, however, entirely conjecture, since Matthew gives us no indication of how long after the nativity the visit of the Wise Men took place. The only thing that is certain is that the Christmas cards and illustrations showing the Magi kneeling in the stable, and hymns which read "as they offered gifts most rare at that manger rude and bare" [4] are completely wrong, for our Lord was in a roofed house when the Wise Men arrived.

The Epiphany was an important festival in Germany in the Middle Ages. The relics of the Magi were transferred from Milan to the Cathedral of Cologne and the day became one of great importance. All Lutheran orders of the sixteenth century kept it as a major festival. Under frontier conditions, and in 1743, when Epiphany fell on a weekday, Henry Melchior Muhlenberg writes: "we celebrated the Festival of the Epiphany in Providence and I preached to the congregation again in the barn." [5]

Because, however, Epiphany falls on a weekday in six years out of every seven, its observance in America is not what it should be. All that many Christians know about it is that it is something that there are Sundays after! Of the major Christian festivals, it is the only one without an important octave. The octave of Easter is Low Sunday; the octave of Pentecost is Trinity Sunday; the octave of Christmas is the Circumcision. Though the last may not fall on a Sunday, it is a holy day of obligation in the Roman Catholic church. But the octave of the Epiphany is completely lost, even in that church. This is all the more to be deplored since the gospel for the octave is

---

[4] William Chatterton Dix, "As with gladness men of old."
[5] Tappert & Doberstein, *op. cit.*, vol. I, p. 84.

the baptism of our Lord—the primitive lesson for the Epiphany, and the gospel which Luther preferred for the festival itself. "Since," he says, "a feast of the manifestation of Christ is celebrated, why not let it be this manifestation, where God the Father and the Son and the Holy Ghost is so strikingly revealed?" [6] The new *Service Book* restores John 1:29-34 as an alternate gospel for the Third Sunday after the Epiphany.

In the Eastern church, the Epiphany emphasis is still on the baptism of Christ. Next to Easter, Epiphany was the season for the reception of candidates by baptism. The ceremony of the blessing of the waters, once entirely religious in character, continues as a kind of folk festival wherever the Eastern church has gone. The clergy proceed to the sea or river, recite a prayer and throw into the water a crucifix which is recovered by swimmers.[7] Since some of the Eastern churches still operate on the old style calendar, this ceremony may take place on January 18.

The period between Christmas and the Epiphany was one of holiday in western Europe. Epiphany was Twelfth Day in England, and its eve furnished the title for one of Shakespeare's best-known plays. The Fridays between Christmas and the Epiphany were exempted from fasting. In medieval England the Monday after Epiphany was "Plough Monday"—the day on which ploughing was begun—and there were prayers for God's blessing upon the tilling and seeding of the land. The octave of the Epiphany, January 13, was marked in France and Germany by the Feast of the Ass (*Eselsfest*).[8] This was a mock

[6] Quoted in Edward T. Horn, *The Christian Year* (Philadelphia: Lutheran Book Store, 1876), p. 60.

[7] In 1954, newspapers carried accounts of this ceremony in Tampa, Florida, and at the Battery in New York harbor. See K. A. Heinrich Kellner, *Heortology*, English translation of the second German edition. (London: Kegan Paul, Trench, Trübner & Co., Ltd., 1908), p. 172.

[8] Alt, *op. cit.*, p. 326. There being no multitude of camels and dromedaries available at Epiphany, asses were substituted. They had a good biblical history including Balaam, the triumphal entry into Jerusalem and the flight into Egypt.

festival in honor of the animals in the stable at Bethlehem. It has left the church a hymn tune, *Orientis partibus,* which covered the procession.

For many centuries the Sundays after the Epiphany had little or no liturgical importance. The season, which may have from one to six weeks, depending upon the date of Easter, is one of the two "accordion pleats" in the church year. The other is the time after Trinity Sunday. A late Easter means a long Epiphanytide and a short Trinity season. If Easter is early, the situation is reversed. In the earlier service books there are from three to ten Sundays after the Epiphany. From the Gregorian Sacramentary on, there have been six. In Roman use, there are propers for only twenty-four Sundays after Pentecost. When there are more than twenty-four Sundays after Pentecost in a given year, the unused Sundays after the Epiphany are used to fill out the church year. In the Anglican use, there are propers provided for twenty-four Sundays after Trinity, and for the Sunday Next before Advent. If there are more than twenty-five Sundays after Trinity, the propers for the Fifth and Sixth Sundays after the Epiphany are used to fill the gap. In Lutheran use, propers are provided for twenty-seven Sundays after Trinity, and it is not necessary to fill out the church year by transposing the unused Epiphany propers.

THE EPIPHANY OF OUR LORD

Like Christmas, the Epiphany is a fixed-date festival, always occurring on January 6. The propers are all historic in the Western church, and are used by both the Roman Catholic and Lutheran churches. The Anglicans have substituted Eph. 3:1-12 for the historic lesson from Isa. 60. The collect is Gregorian, but the Prayer Book translation followed by both Anglicans and Lutherans is defective. The original reads "that we, who know thee now by faith, may be brought to the contemplation of thy Majesty by sight." The phrase "may have the fruition of thy glorious Godhead" is quite obfuscatory.[9] This has been corrected by a new translation in the *Service Book*. The gospel is the visit of the Magi to Bethlehem. A great deal of speculation and much legend has risen regarding them. Actually we are not told that they were three in number, that they were kings, that their names were Caspar, Melchior and Balthasar, or where they came from beyond the indefinite "east." The star, recreated by modern planetariums, seems to have been a conjunction which appeared to the naked eye as a new star of first magnitude. It was this that probably attracted the attention of the Magi who immediately connected it with some great event. The importance of the Epiphany depends not on the details of the story, but on its principal message which concerns the manifestation of Christ to the Gentiles. Because of this, the entire Epiphany season has become a time for emphasis on the missionary task of the Christian church.

> *Propers:* Introit—Liturgical text (*Ecce advenit*);
> Ps. 72:1
> Collect—Gregorian
> Lesson—Isa. 60:1-6
> Epistle—Col. 1:23-27 or Eph. 3:1-12
> Gradual—Isa. 60:6b, 1; Matt. 2:2b
> Gospel—Matt. 2:1-12
> Creed—Nicene
> Proper Preface—Epiphany
> Color—White

THE FIRST SUNDAY AFTER THE EPIPHANY

The collect, epistle, gradual and gospel for this Sunday are the same in Lutheran and Roman use. The introit, which had

---

[9] Massey H. Shepherd, *op. cit.,* p. 108.

an extra-scriptural text, was replaced in Lutheran use by a
scriptural one of parallel thought. The collect is Gelasian.
The epistle marks the beginning of one of the few sequences
that remain of the primitive practice of reading the Bible "in
course" at the services—that is, reading a section and then pick-
ing up and continuing at the next service at the place the
reader had stopped at the previous one. The epistles, none of
which has any particular association with the Epiphany season, continue:

> First Sunday after the Epiphany: Rom. 12:1-5
> Second Sunday after the Epiphany: Rom. 12:6-16a
> Third Sunday after the Epiphany: Rom: 12:16b-21
> Fourth Sunday after the Epiphany: Rom. 13:8-10

The epistle for the First Sunday in Advent, which was often
preceded by the epistle for the Fourth Sunday after the
Epiphany, is Rom. 13:11-14.

There may even be a vestige of an "in course" reading of the
gospels in the Third and Fourth Sundays after the Epiphany,
with Matt. 8:1-13 and Matt. 8:23-27, respectively. The intervening verses deal with Jesus' healing of Peter's mother-in-
law—a lesson which would not be especially popular at Rome.

The gospel for this Sunday is the visit of the child Jesus to
the Temple at the age of twelve, the single glimpse that we
have of the life of our Lord between the flight into Egypt and
the beginning of his ministry nearly thirty years later.

> *Propers:* Introit—Isa. 6:1b; Rev. 19:6; Ps. 100:1, 2a
> Collect—Gelasian
> Lesson—Eccles. 12:1-7
> Epistle—Rom. 12:1-5
> Gradual—Pss. 72:18, 19a, 3; 100:1, 2a

Gospel—Luke 2:41-52
Creed—Nicene or Apostles'
Proper Preface—Epiphany
Color—White

THE SECOND SUNDAY AFTER THE EPIPHANY

The propers for this Sunday are identical in Lutheran and Roman use. The collect and epistle are also in Anglican use, but the American *Book of Common Prayer* has replaced the gospel with Mark 1:1-11, the account of the baptism of Jesus, and has moved this Sunday's gospel to the Third Sunday after the Epiphany. The collect is Gelasian and probably dates from the sixth century. In the original it ends not "grant us thy peace all the days of our life" but "grant us thy peace in our times," an ending which somehow seems more appropriate to the twentieth century than even to the sixth. The gospel recalls one of the earliest associations of the Epiphany season— the changing of water into wine at Cana. At the pagan feast of Dionysus on the night of January 5-6, jars of water were set in the god's temple, the temple doors were sealed, and in the morning it was alleged that the water had become wine. Our Lord's first miracle was probably consciously connected with the Epiphany season to offset this pagan tradition. St. Ambrose, writing in the fourth century, mentions the Magi, the baptism of Jesus, and the miracle at Cana in connection with Epiphany-tide.

In modern Roman practice, the Second Sunday after the Epiphany has, since 1721, been observed as the Feast of the Holy Name of Jesus, and these propers are displaced by those for the newer festival. Instituted by the Franciscans in 1530 with the permission of Pope Clement VII, the Feast of the Holy Name was promoted by St. Bernardine of Siena and, at the request of Emperor Charles VI, was finally added to the official

calendar by Pope Innocent XIII. Since it is of post-Reformation provenance, it has not made its way in Protestant circles,
although there is certainly nothing doctrinally objectionable
about it. The Anglicans have a festival of the Holy Name on
August 7th, but the Lutheran church has continued to follow
the more ancient practice of observing January 1 as a festival
of both the Circumcision and the Name of Jesus.

> *Propers:* Introit—Ps. 66:4, 1, 2
> Collect—Gelasian
> Lesson—Isa. 61:1-6
> Epistle—Rom. 12:6-16a
> Gradual—Pss. 107:20, 21; 148:2
> Gospel—John 2:1-11
> Creed—Nicene or Apostles'
> Proper Preface—Epiphany
> Color—White

THE THIRD SUNDAY AFTER THE EPIPHANY

Lutheran and Roman use agrees in the propers for this
Sunday, with the exception of the Lutheran addition of the
second half of Ps. 97:8 to the introit. The collect is Gelasian,
and the Lutheran use follows the Anglican translation except
for the retention of the phrase "the right hand of thy Majesty"
instead of simply "thy right hand." The gospel is another
narrative of our Lord's manifestation, this time to Jew (the
leper) and Gentile (the Roman centurion) alike.

The new *Service Book* adds, as an alternate gospel, St. John's
account of the baptism of our Lord. In the Western church, this
gospel, which had once belonged to Epiphany Day, was displaced by the story of the Magi. Luther regretted its loss because of its importance as a manifestation of the nature of
Christ.

Propers: Introit—Ps. 97:7b, 8, 1
     Collect—Gelasian
     Lesson—2 Kings 5:1-15
      (end: "but in Israel")
     Epistle—Rom. 12:16b-21
     Gradual—Pss. 102:15, 16; 97:1
     Gospel—Matt. 8:1-13 or John 1:29-34
     Creed—Nicene or Apostles'
     Proper Preface—Epiphany
     Color—White

THE FOURTH SUNDAY AFTER THE EPIPHANY

For this and the succeeding Sundays after the Epiphany, in the Lutheran and Roman systems, the introit and gradual of the Third Sunday after the Epiphany are repeated, since these Sundays do not occur every year, and it is necessary to make up the required number of Sundays after Pentecost (or Trinity) when Easter falls on an early date. The epistle is in both Lutheran and Roman use; the Anglican epistle is Rom. 13:1-7.[10] The gospel in Lutheran and Roman use is the story of the stilling of the tempest on the Sea of Galilee, which is also read (extended through verse 34) in the Anglican churches, except those in America, which use the gospel read in Lutheran and Roman churches on the Third Sunday after the Epiphany. American Episcopalians have omitted this gospel entirely.

Propers: Introit—same as Third Sunday after
     Epiphany
     Collect—Gelasian
     Lesson—Exod. 14:21-31

[10] Massey H. Shepherd, *op. cit.,* p. 114: "It has been suggested that the reason for the substitution was Cranmer's desire to support royal supremacy over the Church in England by providing the classic New Testament passage relating to obedience to civil authority."

Epistle—Rom. 13:8-10
Gradual—same as Third Sunday after
  Epiphany
Gospel—Matt. 8:23-27
Creed—Nicene or Apostles'
Proper Preface—Epiphany
Color—White

THE FIFTH SUNDAY AFTER THE EPIPHANY

This Sunday is used in both Roman and Anglican churches as a "wandering Sunday" to fill in at the end of the season after Pentecost. Some of the early Lutheran orders of the sixteenth century followed this custom. Later sixteenth-century Lutheran orders, however, adopted propers for the closing Sundays of the church year, making it unnecessary to transfer the unused Sundays after the Epiphany to the end of the Trinity season.

The introit and gradual of the Third Sunday after the Epiphany are again repeated. The collect is Gelasian. It appears also in the Missal as the "prayer over the people" (*super populum*), which closes the mass on the Saturday after the Second Sunday in Lent. Its opening clause is the same as the collect for the Twenty-first Sunday after Trinity. The epistle and gospel are the same in Lutheran, Anglican and Roman use. Both of them, but particularly the gospel of the tares and the wheat, reflect the use of the propers for this Sunday at the end of the Trinity season rather than any particular appropriateness for Epiphanytide.

Propers: Introit—same as Third Sunday after
  Epiphany
Collect—Gelasian
Lesson—Ezek. 33:10-16

Epistle—Col. 3:12-17
Gradual—same as Third Sunday after
  Epiphany
Gospel—Matt. 13:24-30
Creed—Nicene or Apostles'
Proper Preface—Epiphany
Color—White

THE SIXTH SUNDAY AFTER THE EPIPHANY

The use of the propers for the Feast of the Transfiguration of our Lord (August 6) as those for the Sixth Sunday after the Epiphany is a Lutheran peculiarity. The Lutheran reformers retained the August 6 date for the festival, but felt that, since its celebration fell on a fixed day (and therefore usually a weekday) and in August, it was worthy of greater consideration in the calendar. Since the Sixth Sunday after the Epiphany was a "wandering Sunday," they displaced the historic propers with those of the Transfiguration. That the Lutheran reformers were not alone in revising this Sunday is indicated by the Anglican appointments which first appeared in the 1662 English Prayer Book, including a collect possibly by Bishop Cosin, 1 John 3:1-8 as the epistle and Matt. 24:23-31 as the gospel. These lessons were not unknown in medieval lectionaries, but their association with this Sunday was. The epistle appeared in some lectionaries for the Eighteenth Sunday after Trinity, for the Epiphany, for Jubilate, and even for Christmas Day. The gospel was used in other lectionaries at the end of the church year, and appears in the Lutheran lectionary as the gospel for the Twenty-fifth Sunday after Trinity. Nor is the Lutheran repetition of the Transfiguration gospel without precedent. In the modern Roman use, this is the gospel for the Second Sunday in Lent, as well as for August 6.

On this Sunday, the Roman and pre-Reformation propers

are: Epistle: 1 Thess. 1:1-10, Gospel: Matt. 13:31-35 (the sin against the Holy Ghost).

The Lutheran use is due to Bugenhagen and Veit Dietrich, liturgical reformers of the sixteenth century. In America, the *Church Book* and the *Common Service Book* went even farther and specified that these propers were to be used on the *last* Sunday after the Epiphany in every year "except when there is only one Sunday after the Epiphany." At the same time, the date of August 6 for the Transfiguration was dropped from the calendar. The new *Service Book* restores the post-Reformation Lutheran use. The propers for Transfiguration will remain for the Sixth Sunday after the Epiphany without the requirement (but with the permission) that they be used on the last Sunday after the Epiphany each year, and August 6 is restored to the calendar as the Feast of the Transfiguration.

> *Propers:* Introit—Pss. 77:18b; 84:1, 2a
> Collect—Roman, fifteenth century
> Lesson—Exod. 34:29-35
> Epistle—2 Pet. 1:16-21
> Gradual—Pss. 45:2a; 110:1; 96:2, 3
> Gospel—Matt. 17:1-9
> Creed—Nicene or Apostles'
> Proper Preface—Epiphany
> Color—White

9.

SEPTUAGESIMA AND
ITS SEASON

The season of Septuagesima, or Pre-Lent, covers three and a half weeks. Its origin is quite obscure. The title appears first in the canons of the Fourth Council of Orleans in 541. Before that time, Quadragesima (forty days) was a term applied to the First Sunday in Lent as well as to the entire Lenten fast. The preceding Sundays were given names by analogy. Quinquagesima is exactly fifty days before Easter—the only one of the Sundays for which the title is precise. Sexagesima is 57 days and Septuagesima 64 days before Easter. The calendar date of Septuagesima depends, of course, upon the date of Easter. It may occur as early as January 18 and as late as February 22.

The season is Roman in origin and its creation may have been influenced by preparatory fasts for monks such as that prescribed by Caesarius of Arles in the sixth century, or by the Lombard invasion of Italy at that time. Whatever its origin, in the Roman Catholic church it represents an extension of Lent over three additional Sundays, with violet vestments, and the omission of both alleluia and the *Gloria in excelsis* from the liturgy, though the latter did not disappear until the eleventh century.

From Rome the season spread over the Western church. In Gaul, however, it had not been accepted by the eighth century when the ceremony of the "farewell to alleluia" still took place on Quinquagesima rather than on the last Sunday after the Epiphany. At this medieval service, an effigy of alleluia was ceremoniously entombed in the chancel while the hymn *Alleluia, dulce carmen* was sung. Alleluia remained buried until the first mass of Easter, when the coffin was opened and alleluia was sung again.[1]

The Lutheran church follows the Roman use in eliminating alleluias from its psalmody in the introits and graduals beginning with Septuagesima, but it retains green as the color of the season, and has so far resisted attempts to extend the already long penitential season of Lent. It does, however, regard all three of these Sundays as major festivals.

The close of the period—from Quinquagesima to Ash Wednesday—has been a period for considerable celebration in anticipation of Lent. In the Middle Ages, carnivals were popular all over Europe on Shrove Tuesday which was known as Fasten's Eve in Scotland, Fastnacht in Germany, and Mardi Gras in France. In Italy masques were worn and folk comedies such as Harlequin and Columbine, Scaramouche and Pantalon, and Punchinello were presented. In Germany the Fastnachtsnarr Hans Wurst presided over the masquerade of gigantic sausages, pretzels and beer kegs. In France the principal attraction was a fattened ox led through the streets to a barbecue. The French influence is perpetuated in the United States in the annual Mardi Gras in New Orleans. In England, the

---

[1] Translated as "Alleluia! song of sweetness"
  Alleluia! Songs of gladness
    Suit not always souls forlorn;
  Alleluia! Sounds of sadness
    'Midst our joyful strains are borne;
  For in this dark world of sorrow
    We with tears our sins must mourn.
  Praises with our prayers uniting,
    Hear us, blessed Trinity;
  Bring us to Thy blissful presence,
    There the Paschal Lamb to see,
  There to Thee our Alleluia
    Singing everlastingly.

pancake is associated with Shrove Tuesday and Shakespeare's clown in *All's Well That Ends Well* remarks, "As fit as a pancake for Shrove Tuesday." In Germany, the doughnut came to symbolize Fastnacht. Both of these customs are believed to have been designed to use up whatever grease might be on hand before Lent began, during which its use was forbidden. Shrove Tuesday gets its name from the shrift, or confession, which was made before Lent began. It is a legal holiday in Louisiana, Alabama and Florida.

SEPTUAGESIMA SUNDAY

The propers for this Sunday are the same in **Lutheran** and Roman use with the exception of the gradual, to which the Lutherans have subjoined the first verse of the tract. The tract is a psalm cento which replaces the gradual alleluia from Septuagesima to the end of Lent. The Lutheran reformers retained the historic graduals, but, with the exception of Palm Sunday and Wednesday in Holy Week, present use limits the tract to a single verse.

The collect is Gelasian and is also in Anglican use, **as is the** gospel. The Anglican epistle was shortened in 1549 to end at 1 Cor. 9:27 instead of continuing to 10:5 as in **Lutheran** and Roman use. The use of the gospel, which is the parable of the laborers and the vineyard, is believed to antedate the season of Septuagesima, and to refer to the spring planting which occurred in southern Europe about this time of the year.

> *Propers:* Introit—Ps. 18:4a, 5a, 6a, 1, 2a
> Collect—Gelasian
> Lesson—Jer. 9:23-24
> Epistle—1 Cor. 9:24—10:5
> Gradual—Pss. 9:9, 10, 18, 19a; 130:1, 2a
> Gospel—Matt. 20:1-16

Creed—Nicene
Proper Preface—none
Color—Green

SEXAGESIMA SUNDAY

This Sunday may originally have been some kind of a com-
memoration of St. Paul, particularly since the propers for the
Festival of SS. Peter and Paul (June 29) all deal with St.
Peter. The stational church for this Sunday is St. Paul's Outside the Walls, on the Ostian Way, where the body of the
Apostle is supposed to be buried. The epistle—the longest
Sunday epistle of the church year—recounts trials and tribula-
tions of St. Paul which would otherwise be unknown to us. The
Latin form of the collect reads "that by thy power we may be
defended against all adversity by the protection of the Doctor
of the Gentiles."

The Lutheran and Roman propers are again identical with
the exception of the tract. In Anglican use the epistle was
shortened in 1549 to end with 2 Cor. 11:31. The gospel—the
parable of the soils, or of the sower—is, like that for Septuagesima, thought to antedate Sexagesima and to have been
selected originally because of its timeliness for the season of
spring planting.

> *Propers:* Introit—Ps. 44:23, 24, 25a, 26a, 1
> Collect—Gelasian
> Lesson—Amos 8:11-12
> Epistle—2 Cor. 11:19—12:9
> Gradual—Pss. 83:18, 13; 60:4
> Gospel—Luke 8:4-15
> Creed—Nicene
> Proper Preface—none
> Color—Green

QUINQUAGESIMA SUNDAY

In many Lutheran orders this Sunday was known by the first words of its Latin introit, *Esto Mihi*. The propers in Lutheran and Roman use are all traditional. The Anglicans use a collect composed for the 1549 Prayer Book, but employ the same epistle and gospel. The epistle, 1 Cor. 13, is a classic of poetic prose and sets forth the ideal of love and its superiority to faith and hope which will one day no longer be needed. The gospel sets the faces of the faithful with our Lord towards Jerusalem and the tragic culminating events of his earthly life. It is an orientation towards Lent which begins on the following Wednesday.

Quinquagesima was, before the extension of the Lenten note to this season, the last Sunday until Easter on which alleluias were sung.

> *Propers:* Introit—Ps. 31:2b, 3, 1
> Collect—Gelasian
> Lesson—Jer. 8:4-9
> Epistle—1 Cor. 13:1-13
> Gradual—Pss. 77:14, 15; 100:1, 2a
> Gospel—Luke 18:31-43
> Creed—Nicene
> Proper Preface—none
> Color—Green

10.

LENT

The origin of Lent lies in two directions: the fast which preceded the Pascha (pas-ka), and the period of preparation prescribed for candidates for baptism. Holy Week seems to have developed from the former; the remainder of Lent from the latter.

The Pascha in the primitive church was a commemoration of the redemption—including both the passion and the resurrection. Following the Jewish custom, the Lord's Day began at 6 P.M. Saturday. But, since Jesus rose from the dead early Sunday morning, Christians fasted until the Eucharist, which was celebrated at about 3 A.M. As late as the early third century the important fast was still restricted to Saturday, according to the *Apostolic Tradition* of Hippolytus, though Friday was sometimes fasted. This was at Rome. By the middle of the century in Syria, according to the *Didascalia,* the fast had been extended to six days. In other places, too, the pre-Pascha fast was gradually extended, first to forty hours (the time our Lord was believed to have spent in the sepulchre), then to the six days before Easter.[1] It was not until the fourth century, however, that the events of Holy Week came to be separated. Some time between 350 and the end of the century, Holy Week, Good Friday and Easter developed at Jerusalem as separate festivals.

[1] The best recent description of this development is in A. Alan McArthur, *op. cit.,* p. 77ff., and especially 114ff.

One of the early features of the services of the Pascha was the baptism of candidates on Saturday night. Membership in the Christian church of the first four centuries was not come by lightly. As an underground organization, the church had to scrutinize carefully every prospective member, and a prolonged period of probation was a requirement. This period would normally terminate with reception into the church by baptism at Easter. The final period preceding baptism was naturally the most rigorous. Candidates were required to fast in preparation, and to attend catechetical lectures and periodic examinations or "scrutinies."

The length of the fast was suggested by our Lord's fast before his ministry began (Matt. 4:2, Luke 4:2), Moses' fast on Sinai (Exod. 24:18, Deut. 9:9), and Elijah's fast on his journey to the Mount of God (1 Kings 19:8), all of which were forty days. In the middle of the fourth century candidates for baptism fasted forty days at Jerusalem, and the catechetical lectures of Cyril of Jerusalem were delivered to them during this period, ending at Easter. The examinations originally began on the Wednesday of the third week of Lent, with the final one on Holy Saturday. Initially there were seven of these scrutinies; by the eighth century they had been reduced to three spread over the six-week period of Lent and falling in the present first, fourth, and last weeks. Some of the epistles still read on Sundays in Lent recall this ancient practice.[2]

After the Edict of Toleration in 313 and the legalizing of Christianity, the scrutinies were relaxed and what had been a period of preparation for baptism became a general period of preparation for all Christians, and while "Lent was not instituted as a historical preparation for the Passion," [3] it soon be-

[2] E.g., the Second Sunday (1 Thess. 4:1-7) bodily purity contrasted with the standards of pagan society; the Third Sunday (Eph. 5:1-9) the "children of disobedience" vs. the "children of light."
[3] A. Alan McArthur, op. cit., p. 129.

came exactly that. Containing, as it did, 36 days of fasting, Lent was thought to represent the "tithe" of the 365 days of the year—a tithe due the Lord in fasting and penance. The addition of the four days from Ash Wednesday to the First Sunday in Lent was made at the end of the seventh or beginning of the eighth century, and these days appear for the first time in the Gelasian Sacramentary. At the same time, the season of Septuagesima takes on the character of a season of preparation for Lent.

The Eastern church has never adopted the Western Lent. By exempting Thursdays and Saturdays, as well as Sundays, from fasting, the Eastern church has an eight-week Lent. Its introduction is graduated. On the Monday after the eighth Sunday before Easter (corresponding to the Western Sexagesima), meat is given up; from the Seventh Sunday (corresponding to Quinquagesima), *lacticinia* (eggs and milk) are given up.

In both East and West the Sundays, being weekly commemorations of the resurrection, were always exempted from the fast. They are not days "of" Lent, even though they are "in" Lent. The Eastern church has maintained this principle better than the Western church. In the East alleluias continue to be sung throughout Lent on Sundays, and the penitential character of the season is confined to the penitential days. In the West the penitential character of the Lenten season has spilled over the Sundays and obscured their true nature as commemorations of the resurrection. This is noticeable in the Roman tracts, which replace the alleluias on Sundays; in the introits; in the omission of the *Gloria in excelsis;* as well as by the use of the penitential color—violet. In many Protestant churches, where the only services held are on Sundays, it is easy to see how this might have occurred; it is difficult to understand, however, in the church of the Middle Ages on any

grounds other than those of the prevailing spirit of the times
and a misunderstanding of the nature of Lent.

Even the days of Lent themselves have too often come to
be dominated by the contemplation of Christ's sufferings and
a sometimes morbid introspection. Occasionally even Roman
Catholic writers are moved to protest this. Writes one, "It is to
be observed further that Lent is not devoted to the consideration of Christ's sufferings. This occupies the mind during Holy
Week. The aim of Lent is not to move the faithful to dwell
upon the passion of Christ, but only to prepare them for keeping Easter worthily. . . . On Palm Sunday for the first time our
thoughts are directed to the Passion in the collect for the day,
while in the prayers for the so-called Passion Sunday it is not
mentioned." [4]

In popular Lutheran use, too, the passion is often extended
throughout the Lenten period. The history of the passion of
our Lord, popular in Germany before the Reformation and
designed originally to be read during Holy Week, is often
read through Lent. Sermons and meditations at midweek
Lenten services are usually concerned with the events and
characters of the passion. Often the result is that, by the time
Holy Week arrives, both people and clergy are weary of the
details of the narrative which is proper to the week before
Easter. As long ago as the fifth century, Leo the Great reminded the faithful in one of his sermons that Lent was appointed to prepare souls for a fruitful commemoration of the
mystery of Easter; as a time of inner purification and sanctifica-
tion, of penance for sins past, of breaking off of sinful habits,
of the exercise of virtues, especially almsgiving, reconciliation
and the laying aside of enmity and hatred.

In the Middle Ages, Lent was marked visibly by the hanging
of the Lenten veil, sometimes called the "hunger veil" because

[4] K. A. Heinrich Kellner, op. cit., pp. 102-3.

of the fast, between the nave and the choir of the churches. The Lenten veil was a necessary reminder to the common man, who had no calendar, that it was Lent. First mentioned in the ninth century, the Lenten veil continued to be used until modern times. In 1552 the church of Boxford, Berkshire, England, had "a lent vayle before the highe awlter wt paynes blewe and white." [5] The veil was hung from Ash Wednesday to Good Friday and was usually drawn aside on Sundays to indicate that they were not part of the fast. The use of the Lenten veil was popular in Westphalia and Hannover, and a similar custom is followed in Russian Orthodox churches.

In the Middle Ages the Sundays in Lent and after Easter were known popularly by the first words of their Latin introits. In the Roman Catholic church in America this custom has survived only in the case of Laetare, but all of the Lenten Sundays bear their Latin titles in the Lutheran church: Invocabit (or Invocavit), Reminiscere, Oculi, Laetare, Judica and Palmarum.[6] The Anglican church dropped the traditional titles altogether and calls the Sundays First, Second, etc., Sundays in Lent.

Since the fourth century Council of Laodicaea, Lent has been a *tempora clausa* during which weddings are discouraged, and cannot be held with a nuptial mass and nuptial blessing. The Roman Catholic church increases its weekly fast by adding the Wednesdays in Lent to the regular Fridays. The Anglicans retain Ash Wednesday and Good Friday as fast days, and the forty days of Lent are listed as "other days of fasting, on which the church requires such a measure of abstinence as is more

---

[5] Walter Money, *Parish Church Goods in Berkshire* (Oxford: Parker, 1879), p. 6.
[6] Mnemonic devices teach the sequence of Sundays to catechumens:

In	Invocabit	I
Richters	Reminiscere	Ran
Ofen	Oculi	Out;
Liegen	Laetare	Let
Jungen	Judica	Jim
Palmen	Palmarum	Pout

especially suited to extraordinary acts and exercises of devotion."
Many of the Lutheran sixteenth-century church orders continued the traditional fast in Lent, such as Brandenburg, 1540,
and Calenberg, 1542. "It is a mistake to suppose that Luther
wished the custom of fasting to be altogether given up." [7] But
in both the Anglican and Lutheran churches fasting was placed
more on an individual basis as, indeed, it had been in the early
centuries of the church's history. The church has always found
fasting to be an excellent means of spiritual discipline, but the
spiritual discipline has been paramount rather than any external
expression of it. The action of Queen Elizabeth I, who, with
the ladies of her court, wore mourning during Lent, was a quite
extreme observance.

For the first six centuries, the church kept Lent free from
saints' days. The first exception was at the Council in Trullo
when the Annunciation was allowed on March 25. This was
followed by many other days in the Western church until the
present Roman calendar lists commemorations on 39 of the
71 days which may fall in Lent.

ASH WEDNESDAY. THE FIRST DAY OF LENT

Ash Wednesday, the beginning of Lent, is forty days (not
counting Sundays) before Easter. It may occur on any date
from February 4 to March 10. The addition of the four days
preceding the First Sunday in Lent was made in sixth-century
Rome, probably to bring the total number of days in the fast
to the forty of that of our Lord. The name "Ash Wednesday"
comes from the medieval custom, continued in the Roman
Catholic church, of sprinkling ashes on the heads of penitents
on this day. Originally these penitents appear to have been
persons under church discipline who wished to be reconciled
to the church on Maundy Thursday. The ashes were a public

[7] Edward T. Horn, *op. cit.,* p. 62.

acknowledgment of their penance. The ashes were prepared by burning the palms of the previous Palm Sunday and pulverizing the ash. Originally the ashes were not blessed, but the penitents were. In the present Roman rite, the ashes are blessed.

As the ceremony of the reconciliation of penitents fell into disuse, the practice arose of marking the heads of all the faithful with an ashen cross as a visible symbol of the penitential season which began on this day. It thus became a general custom no longer confined to those under suspension or excommunication.

The ceremony of the blessing and distribution of the ashes was not retained by the reformers, whether Lutheran, Anglican or Reformed, "not only because of their distaste of the blessing of such things as ashes, but more particularly because the ceremony seemed to be a strange contradiction of the Gospel lesson for the day." [8] The gospel speaks of appearing to fast not to men, but to God alone. The Anglicans did, however, retain the penitential office which preceded the blessing of the ashes in the Sarum rite, as a commination service for use on Ash Wednesday.

The gradual, epistle and gospel are the same in Lutheran and Roman use. The Anglicans use the same gospel but have shortened the epistle by ending it at verse 17. The Lutherans have changed the antiphon to the introit from the apocryphal Wisdom of Solomon to Psalm 57. The collect used by both Lutherans and Anglicans is one prepared for the 1549 English Prayer Book, based upon some of the ancient prayers for the blessing of the ashes in pre-Reformation use. It is a fine prayer of confession and, in the Anglican church, is required to be said daily throughout Lent.

[8] Massey H. Shepherd, *op. cit.*, p. 124.

Propers: Introit—Ps. 57:2, 1b, 1a
　　　　　 Collect—*Book of Common Prayer*
　　　　　　 (I Edward VI) 1549
　　　　　 Lesson—Joel 2:12-19
　　　　　 Epistle—1 John 1:5-9
　　　　　 Gradual—Pss. 57:1a, 3a; 103:10; 79:9
　　　　　 Gospel—Matt. 6:16-21
　　　　　 Creed—Nicene
　　　　　 Proper Preface—Lent
　　　　　 Color—Violet

INVOCABIT. THE FIRST SUNDAY IN LENT

The Sundays in Lent were popularly known in medieval times by the first words of their Latin introits—the opening word of the mass of the day. This Sunday's introit began *Invocabit me, et ego exaudiam eum,* hence the title, Invocabit. The Latin text for the introits and graduals comes from the ancient Itala version of the Bible, which antedated the Vulgate. By a curious error, many Lutheran service books, including the *Common Service Book,* have titled this Sunday Invocavit. "Invocavit" is the perfect tense and would be translated, "he called"; "invocabit" is future and is translated "he shall call." The ninety-first Psalm is entirely future, except for verses 9 and 14a. Possibly the error, which antedates the Reformation and is found in some north European missals, may be due to a copyists confusion of "b" and "v" which are often quite similar in script.

The propers are identical in Lutheran and Roman use, and the Anglicans use the same lessons. They are concerned with the proper orientation of the Christian life and are reminiscent of the early centuries when candidates were under instruction for baptism at Easter. The gospel of the temptation of Christ is one of the oldest assigned lessons, dating back before the time of Leo the Great in the fifth century. The collect is Gelasian and in use except by the Anglicans who have replaced it by a 1549 prayer based on the gospel.

> *Propers:* Introit—Ps. 91:15a, 15c, 16, 1
> Collect—Gelasian
> Lesson—Gen. 22:1-14
> Epistle—2 Cor. 6:1-10
> Gradual—Ps. 91:11, 12, 1
> Gospel—Matt. 4:1-11
> Creed—Nicene
> Proper Preface—Lent
> Color—Violet

REMINISCERE. THE SECOND SUNDAY IN LENT

Like the preceding Sunday, this Sunday takes its name from the opening word of the Latin introit, *Reminiscere miserationum tuarum.* This Sunday follows the Lenten Ember Days when ordinations take place in the Roman Catholic church. It was a "vacant" Sunday without assigned propers. The Roman gospel today is the transfiguration. The epistle is common to Lutheran, Anglican and Roman use and refers to the purity of life expected of the neophytes to be received by baptism at Easter. The gospel, common to both Lutherans and Anglicans, follows north European missals and is the story of the healing of the Syro-Phoenician woman. In the Missal it is read on Thursday of the preceding week. The introit and gradual are taken from the Wednesday Ember Day mass of the preceding week, and are used on this Sunday in both Lutheran and Roman rites. The collect is Gelasian and is used in all three churches.

> *Propers:* Introit—Ps. 25:6, 2b, 22, 1, 2a
> Collect—Gelasian

Lesson—Exod. 33:12-23
Epistle—1 Thess. 4:1-7
Gradual—Pss. 25:17, 18; 107:1
Gospel—Matt. 15:21-28
Creed—Nicene
Proper Preface—Lent
Color—Violet

OCULI. THE THIRD SUNDAY IN LENT

The title comes from the Latin introit, *Oculi mei semper ad Dominum* (Mine eyes are ever toward the Lord). The introit and gradual are in both Lutheran and Roman use. The lessons are common also to the Anglicans, although they have extended the epistle to end at verse 14 instead of 9. Again it recalls the instruction of candidates for baptism in the ancient church when the Third Sunday in Lent was the day of the first "scrutinies" or examinations. This consisted chiefly of exorcisms—the calling out of unclean spirits. The gospel, which is common to all uses and concerns the dumb devil, was undoubtedly selected for its appropriateness. Primitively these exorcisms were performed by one of the now-vanished minor orders of clergy in the church, the exorcists. Gradually, as also happened to the lectors whose privilege had been the public reading of the lessons, their duties passed into the hands of the higher clergy. Exorcism, along with belief in demoniacal possession, has practically disappeared from the church, though a few traces such as this gospel remain. Early titles for this Sunday were *Dominica Abrenuntiationis* (Renunciation Sunday) and *Dominica Exorcismi* (Exorcism Sunday).

Propers: Introit—Ps. 25:15, 16, 1, 2a
Collect—Gregorian
Lesson—Jer. 26:1-15

Epistle—Eph. 5:1-9
Gradual—Pss. 9:19, 3; 123:1, 3a
Gospel—Luke 11:14-28
Creed—Nicene
Proper Preface—Lent
Color—Violet

LAETARE. THE FOURTH SUNDAY IN LENT

The introit for this Sunday begins *Laetare Jerusalem* (Rejoice ye with Jerusalem). The Sunday is also known as Mid-Lent, Refreshment Sunday, Mothering Sunday, *Brotsonntag, Dominica de panibus,* and the Sunday of the Golden Rose. It forms a break in the Lenten fast, as Gaudete (the Third Sunday in Advent) does in Advent. On both Sundays the Roman Catholic church permits the use of rose altar hangings instead of violet, altar flowers and the use of the organ. The title Mid-Lent explains itself. Refreshment Sunday refers to the gospel for the day, the feeding of the five thousand; Mothering Sunday, to the epistle: "Jerusalem which is above is free, which is the mother of us all." In medieval times it was customary to make parochial visits on this Sunday to the "mother" church of the diocese. In England, a popular folk custom was for servants and apprentices, who could seldom get home, to visit their mothers on this day, taking as a present a "mothering cake" or "simnel." [9] In a sense, Laetare is the first Mother's Day!

The titles *Brotsonntag* and *Dominica de panibus* refer to the

[9] Maskell, *op. cit.,* vol. III, p. 48fn. The king presented simnels to the monks of Westminster following his coronation. "It is to be hoped that, whatever they were made of, they were more tempting to look at than simnels of the present day, which are really offensive in their appearance; and cannot but be, as another old writer, Constantius Africanus has described them, 'very indigestible' although possibly 'very nutritious.' We must commiserate the daily fare of the convent of Westminster when simnels, such as these, were an extraordinary treat. . . . The town of Devizes in Wiltshire has long been famous for these simnels and at present they are made of flour, yeast, saffron, currants and spice. They are first boiled, and afterwards baked."

ancient custom, inspired by the day's gospel, of the pope's distribution of bread to the poor on Laetare. Among the Slovaks and Wends a folk festival on Laetare symbolized the end of winter and the birth of spring.[10] The Sunday of the Golden Rose, or Rose Sunday, referred to the medieval custom of the award by the pope of the Golden Rose to churches, Roman Catholic rulers or other persons of distinction, governments or cities, for conspicuous service to the Roman church and the Holy See. The Golden Rose, even though it might not be awarded each year, was blessed each year on Laetare. Henry VIII received the Golden Rose on three different occasions from three different popes! In America, a relic of this custom remains in the annual award by Notre Dame University, South Bend, Indiana, of a medal to the outstanding Roman Catholic layman of the year. The medal is known as the Laetare Medal.

The propers for the day are identical in Lutheran and Roman use. The Anglican church ends the epistle at Gal. 4:31 instead of adding 5:1a, "stand fast therefore in the liberty wherewith Christ hath made us free," and ends the gospel at verse 14 instead of 15. The new Lutheran *Service Book* restores to the epistle Gal. 5:1a, which was unfortunately excised by the reformers, both Lutheran and Anglican.

> *Propers:* Introit—Isa. 66:10; Ps. 122:1
> Collect—Gelasian
> Lesson—Isa. 55:1-7
> Epistle—Gal. 4:21—5:1a
> Gradual—Ps. 122:1, 7; 125:1
> Gospel—John 6:1-15
> Creed—Nicene
> Proper Preface—Lent
> Color—Violet

[10] Alt, *op. cit.,* p. 110.

JUDICA. PASSION SUNDAY

Like the preceding Sundays in Lent, this Sunday gets its title from the first word of the Latin introit, *Judica me.* Passion Sunday is a secondary title found in north European missals, though the Roman title is *Dominica de Passione.* Passion Week, which is the week following Passion Sunday, and is not to be confused with Holy Week, is a term which originated in nineteenth-century Anglicanism. The English church marked off the last two weeks of Lent as of special significance. The altar colors at Westminster, for instance, in medieval times were black for the first four weeks in Lent, and red for the last fortnight.[11] This change was also made in some parts of the continent. At Ellwangen, Württemberg, the color was white to the octave of the Epiphany, then violet until Septuagesima, black from Septuagesima to Passion Sunday, and red for Passiontide, including Maundy Thursday.[12]

The lessons and collect are the same in Lutheran, Anglican and Roman uses. The introit and gradual are in both Lutheran and Roman use.

> *Propers:* Introit—Ps. 43:1, 2a, 3a
> Collect—Gelasian
> Lesson—Num. 21:4-9
> Epistle—Heb. 9:11-15
> Gradual—Pss. 143:9a, 10a; 18:48; 129:1, 2
> Gospel—John 8:46-59
> Creed—Nicene
> Proper Preface—Lent
> Color—Violet

[11] Vernon Staley, *The Ceremonial of the English Church, op. cit.,* pp. 243-44.
[12] Joseph Braun, *op. cit.,* p. 45.

11.

HOLY WEEK

Holy Week begins with Palm Sunday. The week is older than Lent and was one of the sources from which Lent later developed. Its origin lies in the ceremonies of the Pascha in the primitive church, and the gradual extension of the preparatory period. In fourth-century Jerusalem, Holy Week really came into its own, when the events of the week could be re-enacted with ceremonies at or near the sites of their actual occurrence. Holy Week is really subdivided into two parts, of which the *Triduum* (three days), i.e., Maundy Thursday, Good Friday and Holy Saturday, is the more solemn, but the entire week is of special importance.

One of the ancient characteristics of the devotions of the week was the reading of the passions of our Lord from the Four Gospels. The Mozarabic rite (Spanish) had a cento from the Four Gospels which was read on Good Friday, but the medieval and current Roman use has been to read the Passion according to St. Matthew (chapters 26 and 27) on Palm Sunday; the Passion according to St. Mark (chapters 14 and 15) on Tuesday; the Passion according to St. Luke (chapters 22 and 23) on Wednesday; and the Passion according to St. John (chapters 18 and 19) on Good Friday. In the Middle Ages, these readings were intoned; parts were assigned to different cantors and the choir, and the readings gradually assumed a dramatic and musical quality. These ceremonies did not cease at the Reformation but continued to develop in Germany and in the Lutheran church. Bach's *St. Matthew's Passion* is the musical culmination of this practice, and passion plays such as the world-famous one at Oberammergau are the end product of the dramatic development.

Because of the repetition of many of the events of the passion in the four different accounts, there developed in the Middle Ages a conflation of the Four Gospels into one account. There were many such "histories of the passion." Some of them were quite ingenious. Sometimes they were read dramatically; sometimes chorales and meditations were interspersed with the reading. In many parts of the Lutheran church the popularity of these syntheses displaced the straight reading of the four passions, and most Lutheran service books still contain, for reading during Holy Week, a "History of the Passion of our Lord according to the Four Evangelists." This history is often divided into seven parts, one of which is to be read on each day of the week. The most popular is one based on a passion history by Bugenhagen, which many sixteenth-century Lutheran orders specified for use at matins and vespers on the days of Holy Week. The best of these conflations, however, is open to serious criticism. There is a large amount of subjective judgment, particularly as to the precise sequence of minor events, and in choices made among varying accounts of major ones. The Lutheran church is gradually returning to the historic reading of the four passions, and the new *Service Book* restores them as the proper lessons for their respective days.

In England and some places in Europe, Holy Week was marked off visibly from the rest of Lent by the use of red altar colors. This was true at Westminster Abbey, Bath and Wells, and Lichfield in England, and in Ellwangen, Württemberg. Since not many color sequences have come down to us from medieval times, it seems safe to conclude that this use was quite widespread.

PALMARUM. THE SIXTH SUNDAY IN LENT

In Lutheran use, this is the only Sunday in Lent that does not take its title from the first word of the introit, though it was once called *Dominica Osannae* (Hosanna Sunday). In Roman use, Hosanna is the first word of the office for the blessing of the palms which precedes the mass. The title Palm Sunday does not appear in its title at all in Lutheran service books, and has appeared in Anglican use only since 1928. The word *Palmarum* means "of the palms" and refers to the medieval ceremony of the blessing of the palms and the procession which followed. These ceremonies are still observed in the Roman Catholic church.

Where possible, following the blessing of the palms and their distribution to the people, a double-file procession of clergy and congregation forms, each person holding his palm in his outer hand. The procession goes outside the church, the church doors are then closed, and the procession returns to the door. The choir sings the stanzas of the hymn, *Gloria laus et honor* (All glory, laud, and honor), and the congregation joins in the refrain. At the end of the hymn, the subdeacon strikes the church door with the lower end of the staff of the processional cross; the door is opened and the procession re-enters the church. When or where it is impossible to go outside the church, the ceremony takes place inside at the entrance to the chancel.

The procession is in imitation of the triumphal entry of our Lord into Jerusalem. In fourth-century Jerusalem, when the Christian church was first permitted to operate in public, the faithful gathered on the Mount of Olives and, with waving palm branches, escorted the bishop astride an ass, into the city. As in many other instances, this ceremony was adapted at Rome in the sixth century, though the earliest sacramentaries have nothing about the blessing of the palms and the procession.

The earliest prayers—like those on Ash Wednesday—are not for the blessing of the palms but for the blessing of those who carried them. The first trace of the blessing of palms at Rome appears in the ninth century, and it is thought that both the blessing of the palms and their distribution probably originated in Gaul in the eighth century. In the Eastern church there is no procession, but the worshipers hold palms in their hands during the service.

The Protestant reformers, who objected to the blessing of things, did not retain the blessing of the palms, though the procession was retained in some places, e.g., Brandenburg, 1540. Many Lutheran orders did retain the distribution of the palms. Other German customs have died out, particularly the naive processions on Palm Sunday in the Middle Ages in which a wooden figure of our Lord seated on an ass was brought into the church and venerated by clergy and people during the singing of hymns. These "palmesels" exist today only in museums.

In the ancient church, before the association of this Sunday with the palms and the procession, the Sunday was called *Dominica competentium,* or, in the Gallican Missal, *Missa in Traditio Symboli.* These titles refer to the preparation of candidates for baptism at Easter. The *competentes* or cate- chumens under instruction learned the creed for the first time in a ceremony known as the *traditio symboli.* After a few introductory remarks by the priest, a member of one of the minor orders of the clergy rehearsed the candidates in the creed. This seems odd to twentieth-century Christians who are in- structed in the creed and its meaning quite carefully well in advance of admission to the church. In the early church, how- ever, the creed was regarded as one of the secrets of the faith and was revealed only to those in the last stages of their instruc- tion. The same thing was true of the Lord's Prayer, which was not taught candidates until immediately *after* their baptism!

The introit, gradual and collect are common to Lutheran and Roman use. The epistle is used by Anglicans as well, as is the collect. For the gospel, the Roman use and the alternate Lutheran use, is the Passion according to St. Matthew, chapters 26 and 27. The alternate Lutheran gospel, Matt. 21:1-9, is the gospel from the office of the blessing of the palms. It is the same as the gospel for the First Sunday in Advent. It is still used in the Roman Catholic church as the last gospel on Palm Sunday at all low masses.[1] The Anglicans use Matt. 27:1-54 as the gospel, having transferred Matt. 26 to Morning Prayer on Palm Sunday.

> *Propers:* Introit—Ps. 22:19, 21, 1a
> Collect—Gelasian
> Lesson—Zech. 9:9-12
> Epistle—Phil. 2:5-11
> Gradual—Pss. 73:23b, 24, 1; 22:1a, 4a, 5a
> Gospel—Matt. 21:1-9 or 26:1—27:66[2]
> Creed—Nicene
> Proper Preface—Lent
> Color—Violet

MONDAY IN HOLY WEEK

Down at least to the time of Leo the Great (fifth century) there were no services on Monday and Tuesday in Holy Week. Leo's homily on the passion was begun on Palm Sunday and continued on Wednesday. The Passion according to Matthew was assigned to Palm Sunday; Luke to Wednesday and John to

---

[1] Missale Romanum: "In Missis privatis legitur in fine Evang. Cum appropinquasset Jesus, ut supra in benedictione Palmarum."

[2] There is much evidence for the anointing at Bethany (Mark 14:3-9) as an ancient gospel for Palm Sunday. Muhlenberg writes in 1742 (*Journals, op. cit.,* I, p. 18): "On Palm Sunday . . . heard the Rev. Mr. Butjenter preach to my edification on the text Mark 14, where our blessed Saviour was anointed in Bethany."

Friday. Mark was not used anciently. The second Gospel was not highly regarded in medieval times, and was long thought to be only an abbreviation of Matthew. Later, Mark was assigned to Tuesday, leaving Monday without a passion. This is still the case in Lutheran and Roman use.

The Anglican church has reassigned the four passions, dividing each of them in two parts. Matt. 26 is read at morning prayer on Palm Sunday, and chapter 27 at communion (to verse 54). Mark 14 is read on Monday; chapter 15 on Tuesday. Luke 22 is read on Wednesday; chapter 23 on Thursday; John 18 at morning prayer on Good Friday; chapter 19 at the antecommunion. This reassignment dates from 1662; the First Prayer Book of Edward VI (1549) retained the historic arrangement.

The introit, collect, epistle and gradual are identical in Lutheran and Roman use (except for the tract). The Roman gospel, John 12:1-9 (the Anointing at Bethany) has been extended in Lutheran use to John 12:1-36.[3] The American Anglican propers are all new. The collect was written by Bishop Huntington and adopted in 1928; the epistle is Isa. 3:1-19 and dates from 1549; the gospel is Mark 14.

> *Propers:* Introit—Ps. 35:1, 2, 3
> Collect—Gelasian
> Lesson—Isa. 50:5-10
> Epistle—1 Peter 2:21-24
> Gradual—Pss. 35:23, 3a; 79:9
> Gospel—John 12:1-36
> Creed—Nicene
> Proper Preface—Lent
> Color—Violet

---

[3] There is precedent for this lesson in north European missals, e.g., Sarum. The lesson seems to have been verses 1-36 originally and to have been gradually reduced to the present Roman use.

TUESDAY IN HOLY WEEK

The introit, collect, epistle, gradual and gospel are the same in Lutheran and Roman use. As an alternate to the Passion according to St. Mark, Lutheran use permits the continuation of Monday's gospel, John 12:37-50. These Johannine gospels provide the background for John 13:1-15, which is the gospel for Maundy Thursday. The Anglican collect is again a modern one (1928); the assigned epistle is Isa. 50:5-11, and the gospel is Mark 15, the second half of St. Mark's Passion.

> *Propers:* Introit—Gal. 6:14; Ps. 67:1
> Collect—Gelasian
> Lesson—Jer. 11:18-20
> Epistle—1 Tim. 6:12-14
> Gradual—Ps. 35:13, 1a, 2
> Gospel—John 12:37-50 or
> Mark 14:1—15:46
> Creed—Nicene
> Proper Preface—Lent
> Color—Violet

WEDNESDAY IN HOLY WEEK

The Roman Missal assigns two Old Testament lessons to this day: Isa. 62:11—63:7 and Isa. 53:1-12. The former of these is retained in Lutheran use on this day, with an alternate choice of Isa. 52:13—53:3. The introit, collect, gradual and gospel are the same. The collect, which is Gelasian, bears a striking resemblance to the collect for Laetare. The American Anglican propers include a 1928 collect, Heb. 9:16-28 as the epistle, and the first half of St. Luke's Passion as the gospel.

> *Propers:* Introit—Phil. 2:10, 8b, 11b; Ps. 102:1
> Collect—Gelasian

Lesson—Isa. 62:11—63:7 or
   Isa. 52:13—53:3
Epistle—Rev. 1:5b-7
Gradual—Pss. 69:17, 1, 2a; 102:1, 13
Gospel—Luke 22:1—23:53
Creed—Nicene
Proper Preface—Lent
Color—Violet

THURSDAY IN HOLY WEEK

Thursday in Holy Week, as most Lutheran service books call it, or Maundy Thursday, as it is known elsewhere in the Christian church, is the anniversary of the institution of the Lord's Supper. In one of the oldest calendars it is called *Natalis Calicis* (Birthday of the Chalice), and this name was used in Gaul in the sixth and seventh centuries. In Germany the day is *Gründonnerstag* (Green Thursday) from the green vestments formerly worn at the mass of the day. In some Lutheran books and orders (e.g., Hamburg 1529), it is called Holy Thursday, though that title is customarily associated with Ascension Day. The name Maundy Thursday is derived from the foot-washing ceremony, performed in imitation of our Lord's action at supper and of his subsequent *mandatum* (new commandment), from which the word "maundy" is coined. The foot washing is still continued in the Church of the Brethren, and the Roman Catholic church has restored the practice to general usage wherever local authorities deem it appropriate. At least one sixteenth-century Lutheran order (Brandenburg 1540) continued the custom. In England, the kings and queens down to James II performed the rite on Maundy Thursday. After James II, the King's Almoner (the Archbishop of York) continued the ceremony until the reign of

Queen Victoria, since when it has been replaced by an increased contribution by the crown to the poor.

In the Middle Ages the ceremonies of Maundy Thursday began on Wednesday evening with a service known as Tenebrae.[4] Tenebrae consisted of a number of psalms, after the reading of each of which a candle was extinguished until, after the concluding psalm and prayers, the church was in complete darkness. Following Tenebrae came the rite of the reconciliation of penitents. These were persons who had been barred from the fellowship of the church (excommunicated) and had, since Ash Wednesday, been doing penance. At the service of reconciliation they prostrated themselves while the miserere and prayers were said, after which they received absolution and remained to receive communion with the rest of the congregation. In many places there were two communions on Maundy Thursday—the first in the morning, and the other, in commemoration of the Last Supper, in the evening. Until 1952, when the Roman Catholic church relaxed its regulations, Maundy Thursday was the only day on which an evening mass was allowed.

In the afternoon, the foot washing was performed. Sometimes the bishop washed the feet of twelve old men, representing the Apostles. In monastic communities the abbot washed the feet of the monks. Oil was consecrated on Maundy Thursday for use throughout the diocese during the coming year in baptisms, confirmations, extreme unctions and exorcisms. This rite was known as the consecration of the chrism. In some parts of Europe, the candidates for Easter baptism, who had been given the creed on Palm Sunday, now recited it publicly to the congregation in a ceremony known as the *redditio symboli.* In Rome, however, this was done on Saturday in Holy Week.

---

[4] Literally "darkness" or "shadows." These services were sometimes called "dark matins."

As part of the later communion service, a special host was blessed and consecrated for use on Good Friday at the Mass of the Presanctified. This host was then escorted in procession to a side altar known as the Altar of Repose. And following the communion service, the altars were stripped and washed in preparation for the austere services of Good Friday.

In the later Middle Ages—from the fifteenth century on—the papal bull *in Coena Domini* was read. This was a general excommunication of all heretics. By the sixteenth century it included Hussites, Wyclifites, Lutherans, Zwinglians, Calvinists, Huguenots, Anabaptists, Antitrinitarians and all apostates in general. Of it Luther remarked in his *Table Talk:* "At Rome they wait all year for Maundy Thursday, when Christ instituted the Holy Supper, to damn the heretics, of whom I, Martin Luther, am first and foremost. This happens on the very day when men should be thanking God for his great goodness in the Lord's Supper and his suffering and death. But there sits the pope on high; the cardinals light the torch and all the banned are consigned to hell. I have been in hell for twenty-eight years—since 1518—and I'm still quite hearty in spite of it." [5] The reading of the bull was dropped in Germany after the sixteenth century, but was continued in some places until the end of the eighteenth.[6]

Most of the medieval ceremonies of Maundy Thursday are continued in the modern Roman Catholic church where the *Gloria in excelsis* is used at mass; bells are permitted; and the altar color is white.[7]

---

[5] Quoted in Alt, *op. cit.,* p. 357f. The bull began: "Excommunicamus et anathematizamus ex parte Dei omnipotentis Patri et Filii et Spiritus S., auctoritate quoque beatorum Apostolorum Petri et Pauli ac nostra: quoscunque Hussitas, Wiclefitas, Lutheranos, Zwinglianos, Calvinistas, Ugonottas, Anabaptistas. . . ."

[6] Kellner, *op. cit.,* p. 73.

[7] For the description of modern Roman ceremonies of Maundy Thursday, cf. Adrian Fortescue, *The Ceremonies of the Roman Rite Described, op. cit.,* p. 275ff.

The introit for the day is the same as for Tuesday in Holy Week, and is, along with the gradual, identical in Lutheran and Roman use. The Roman collect, which sets forth the Roman doctrine of the mass, was quite unacceptable to the reformers. The Anglicans provide a modern collect. The Lutheran use is the collect composed by St. Thomas Aquinas in 1264 for the then new Feast of Corpus Christi.[8] The epistle, common to all, is the earliest written account of the institution of the Lord's Supper, antedating the gospel accounts. The Anglicans use only verses 23-26, instead of 20-32. The gospel —the maundy, or foot washing—is also common to all, though both Anglicans and Lutherans permit an alternate. The Anglican alternate is the second half of St. Luke's Passion (chapter 23). The Lutheran alternate is the very appropriate "I am the bread of life" passage from John 6, which, since the foot washing has become obsolete in the Lutheran church, has more relevance in our time.

>   *Propers:* Introit—same as Tuesday in Holy Week
>   Collect—St. Thomas Aquinas, 1264
>   Lesson—Exod. 12:1-14
>   Epistle—1 Cor. 11:20-32
>   Gradual—Phil. 2:8b, 9
>   Gospel—John 13:1-15 or John 6:28-37
>   Creed—Nicene
>   Proper Preface—Lent
>   Color—Violet

GOOD FRIDAY

Like the other separate observances of Holy Week, Good Friday, as a separate day, developed in fourth-century Jerusalem.

[8] The Scottish *Book of Common Prayer* (1929) has followed this use by providing this collect as an alternate.

There is no Good Friday, as such, in the *Apostolic Tradition* of Hippolytus, written in third-century Rome, or in the writings of Tertullian in the same period in North Africa. But the pilgrim Etheria, visiting Jerusalem after the middle of the fourth century, found a full religious observance of Good Friday.[9] Prior to the fourth century, however, what is now Good Friday was part of the fast which preceded the Pascha— the single festival which commemorated the redemption, and which began at sundown on Saturday. By the middle of the third century this fast had been extended to the 40 hours from the time our Lord was crucified until his resurrection. Yet, even at this early date, the latter part of the fast—on Saturday— was the more important.

When Good Friday emerged as a separate day commemorative of the crucifixion and death of Jesus, it became at once the church's great day of mourning and therefore of fasting. Since then, in all lands and in all periods of Christian history, there has been agreement on the nature of Good Friday as on almost no other day in the calendar. In liturgical churches, the color of the day has been black.

The ancient title for the day was *Parasceve* (Preparation). The name Good Friday is of English origin and is possibly derived from "God's Friday" just as "good-bye" is derived from "God be with you."

In the Middle Ages the observances of Good Friday began with Tenebrae on Thursday evening. The service of the day itself was austere, beginning with the prostration of the celebrant before the altar and the reading, without announcement, of lections from the Old Testament and the Passion according to St. John. Then followed what Lutherans know as the Bidding Prayer—a series of "bids" read by a deacon, followed by a moment of silence, and then a collect read by the celebrant.

[9] Cf. McArthur, *op. cit.,* p. 87.

The Bidding Prayer is of particular interest since it is probably the prototype of all so-called "general prayers." In the days when Christian worship was in Greek (until about the fourth century, when it was first Latinized in North Africa), this prayer was part of the normal Sunday service. When the service was translated into Latin, it was removed from the service, and was retained only in the devotions for Good Friday. That it did not always belong here is indicated by the fact that there is nowhere in it any reference to the passion— a surprising omission had the prayer been originally intended for use on Good Friday.

Following the Bidding Prayer, the rite of the Adoration of the Cross is performed with accompanying reproaches and hymns. The host which was consecrated on Maundy Thursday is then brought from the Altar of Repose and the priest and people receive communion.

Many of these rites are of late medieval provenance. The early Good Friday services were much simpler. They agree in one item: there was no communion on Good Friday—and this is still true in the Eastern church. The Gelasian and old Gallican sacramentaries provide no masses for Good Friday, but simply prayers. The Adoration of the Cross seems to have originally been a separate afternoon or vesper service, which had its origin in Jerusalem in the fourth century, and reached Rome in the seventh or eighth century. The first mention of the Mass of the Presanctified is in the eighth century.

The reformers generally eliminated most of these features of the medieval services. The Lutheran church retained the Bidding Prayer, but both Lutherans and Anglicans discarded the Adoration of the Cross and the Mass of the Presanctified. In some parts of the Lutheran church where there was strong Calvinistic influence, there developed a custom of communion on Good Friday which was not known to the other Lutheran church orders of the sixteenth century. While the *Book of Common Prayer* contains no rubric forbidding Good Friday communion, it is rare in Anglican circles. Henry Melchior Muhlenberg did not practice Good Friday communion, but the day was rather one of penance and preparation for the Easter communion. In 1748 he writes, "Good Friday. I . . . preached on the fourth word from the cross, and had preparatory service and confession." [10]

In medieval times it was often customary to entomb in churches a figure of Christ, or a crucifix, or a cross to be "resurrected" on Easter.[11] Even churches which did not entomb anything had replicas of a sepulchre which were set up on Good Friday and removed before the first service of Easter. This custom continues in the Eastern church. In England, a peculiar ceremony was the blessing of "cramp rings" by the king in his chapel. These rings were supposed to cure cramps and were efficacious because of "the special gift of curation ministered to the kings of this realm." [12] Another popular belief was that bread baked on Good Friday was a panacea, and that a few crumbs of it would cure practically anything. In England this bread became in time the hot cross bun. The day was also the occasion of passion plays in many towns and villages—a custom still continued in Mexico,[13] and several other Latin countries.

In the Roman Missal the propers include no introit, the collect for Maundy Thursday which the reformers rejected, Hos. 6:1-6 and Exod. 12:1-11, no gradual but a lengthy tract from Psalm 140, and the Passion according to St. John. The

---

[10] Tappert and Doberstein, *op. cit.,* vol. I, p. 188.
[11] The custom of burying the cross dates from the tenth century.
[12] Cf. Maskell, *op. cit.,* vol. III, pp. clviii-clix. "Lord Berners . . . when ambassador to the emperor Charles V, wrote from Saragossa 'to my lorde cardinall's grace' in 1518 for some 'crampe rynges, with trust to bestow them well, with God's grace.'" The Order for the Blessing of the Rings is in Maskell, vol. III, pp. 335-40.
[13] New York *Times,* March 8, 1953, lists the best at Extrapalapa near Mexico City, and at Tzintzuntzon in Hichoacan.

Lutherans use an introit and gradual based on Isaiah 53 which is also the basis of the tract in the Roman Mass of the Passion, Isa. 53:4-12 or Hos. 6:1-6, and the Passion according to St. John. Both Lutherans and Anglicans have for the collect a Gelasian collect used as the closing prayer *super populum* in the Missal on Wednesday in Holy Week. To this the Anglicans have added the collect for "all estates of men" from the Bidding Prayer, and a 1549 collect. As an epistle they read Heb. 10:1-25. The first half (chapter 18) of the St. John Passion is read at Morning Prayer; chapter 19 is read at the antecommunion. This division of the passion was made in 1662.

> *Propers:* Introit—Isa. 53:4a, 5a, 6a, 6c; Ps. 102:1
> Collect—Gelasian
> Lesson—Isa. 53:4-12 or Hos. 6:1-6
> Epistle—Rev. 5:1-14
> Gradual—Isa. 53:5, 11a
> Gospel—John 18:1—19:42
> Creed—Nicene
> Proper Preface—Lent
> Color—Black

SATURDAY IN HOLY WEEK

Saturday in Holy Week, called anciently "The Great Sabbath" or "Holy Saturday" (*Sabbato Sancto*) was once characterized by a number of interesting ceremonies culminating in the baptism of the candidates who had been under scrutiny during Lent, and the first Easter service, held during the night at about the time when our Lord was believed to have risen from his grave. The Protestant reformers eliminated these ceremonies, again (as on Ash Wednesday, Palm Sunday and Good Friday) largely because of their aversion to the blessing of things, rather than for any serious doctrinal difficulties.

Initially Easter began, following the Jewish reckoning used in the primitive church, at sundown on Saturday. The services commenced then with a vigil (*pervigilum paschale*) spent in prayer and meditation, followed by the baptism of the neophytes who then received their first communion at the first mass of Easter which took place towards dawn.

As time passed, the ceremonies came to be elaborated and to be moved forward from sundown on Saturday to earlier in the day. By the time of the Gelasian Sacramentary the baptismal candidates met early in the morning for their final exorcisms, the renunciation of Satan, and, at Rome, for the public recital of the creed. In the afternoon at the eighth hour (2 P.M.) following the litany, the paschal candle was blessed and lighted, the Old Testament lessons were read, each being followed by a prayer, and the font was blessed, followed by the baptisms and the first Easter service. At a later date, still other ceremonies were added, such as the blessing of new fire and of incense. The ceremonies of the day now began, as on the two preceding days, with Tenebrae on the previous (Friday) evening, at which once more a candle was extinguished following the reading of each of the many tenebrae psalms. The lighting of the paschal candle is of ancient provenance. No one knows quite when or where it began, but tradition ascribes the composition of the *exsultet,* the beautiful chant sung at the blessing of the candle, to St. Augustine in the fourth century. The ancient name for those about to be baptized was *illuminandi,* and it is not surprising to find an early association between the light given the newly-baptized and the symbol of the paschal candle. This candle, of heroic size, was then placed on its own candlestick near the altar and lighted at each mass from Easter to Ascension Day.

The blessing of new fire appears to have some connection with a practice known to have taken place at vespers in the primitive church, when the candles were lighted and the ancient hymn, *Phos hilaron* (Hail, gladdening light), was sung. There may also be some connection with the pagan *Osterfeuer* of the ancient Germans. The ceremony came into Roman use at the time of Leo IV in the ninth century, at a time when many Gallican customs were adopted at Rome.

At present, in Roman use, all of these ceremonies take place on Saturday morning so that the ancient first mass of Easter is actually celebrated on the day before Easter. Some idea of the ancient practice may still be found in the Eastern churches. There the vigil is still observed with the last devotions of Lent —the people prostrating themselves before the tomb set up in the front of the church. Just before midnight the procession forms to go out of the church, with the clergy and people bearing the sacred vessels, books and banners. While the procession perambulates the church to the accompaniment of the church bells, the tomb is removed, candles replaced and the altar dressed for the first mass of Easter, which begins with the triumphant entry of the procession at midnight.

The custom of Easter baptisms, while it persists to some extent, is not what it once was. In ancient times baptisms were held only on this day (and in the East on Epiphany) and, for special cases, on the Saturday before Pentecost. With the rise in infant baptism, however, it became customary to baptize soon after birth and from the sixth century on the importance of the Easter baptisms declined. One of the interesting items lost to use was an anniversary service—the *pascha annotina*— for all the baptized. It was the ancient prototype of the "confirmation reunion." All those baptized at Easter renewed their baptismal vows and engaged in special thanksgivings and prayers. When candidates ceased being baptized on the same day, this special service lost its significance, although the Roman

Catholic church has recently restored to the Easter Vigil service the renewal of baptismal vows.

In many Latin countries, the day is one of celebration—partly to make up for the restraint of Good Friday, and partly because Easter has practically been moved forward to Saturday morning. Effigies of Judas filled with fireworks and burned in the public squares, are still a popular feature of the day in Mexico and South America. In Protestant areas, however, the end of Lent is not anticipated, and the celebration of Easter is reserved for Easter Day. Holy Saturday or Easter Eve is still part of the three days our Lord spent in the grave.

Because of the anticipation of Easter and the advancing of the first mass of Easter, the reformers had to find new propers for the day. The Anglican propers are all from 1549 or later. The only Lutheran item that is ancient is the collect, which comes from the Gelasian Sacramentary.

> *Propers:* Introit—Ps. 130:6a, 5, 1, 2a
> Collect—Gelasian
> Lesson—Exod. 13:17-22
> Epistle—1 Pet. 3:17-22
> Gradual—Pss. 16:9b, 10a; 31:5, 1a
> Gospel—Matt. 27:57-66
> Creed—Nicene
> Proper Preface—Lent
> Color—Violet

12.

EASTER AND ITS SEASON

Easter Day is the oldest and, in a sense, the source of all the festivals of the Christian year. The earliest reference to any church season is to the period of fifty days begun with Easter and ended with Pentecost. Older than Advent and Lent, it was called the *Quinquagesima*—the Holy Fifty Days, or the Great Fifty Days. The ancient name for Easter was Pascha which is derived from the Hebrew word meaning "passover." The title Easter is derived from the Anglo-Saxon spring goddess, Eostre, whose festival occurred each year at the vernal equinox.

Easter and its note of joy and triumph dominated the spirit of the primitive Christian church to an extent difficult for modern Christians to realize or recapture. The resurrection was the impetus for the missionary activity of the early preachers and the keynote of their sermons. The weekly celebration of the resurrection was the reason for the dedication of the first day of the week, Sunday, to Christian worship. Even persecution and martyrdom could not rob the early church of the dominant spirit of the new faith typified in the joy of the resurrection.

The ancient church recognized this spirit in the special nature of the Easter season. The church year began with the Pascha, as it still does in the Eastern churches. Every Sunday between Easter and Pentecost was a major festival. There was no kneeling at the services during the Great Fifty Days. There were no fast days from Easter to Pentecost. Its dominant note was caught in the "alleluia" (the Hebrew shout of joy meaning "praise the Lord"), which spilled over from the services of the Pascha into all the services of the church. It was only much later, during the Dark Ages, that Lent began to usurp the place once held by the Easter season; the miserere began to displace alleluia; man became more concerned with his own lost condition than with God's redemption. Customs are hard to change, but it would be well if the church could come out of its medieval bondage to Lent into the promised land of Easter triumph where it once dwelt in the long ago.

Initially the entire season of fifty days from Easter to Pentecost was observed as one continuous festival. It was not until the fourth century that the historical sequence of events of the season began to be separated and celebrated successively: the Resurrection, the Ascension, Pentecost. This separation of the festival into its component parts took place at Jerusalem. The precedent for the single commemoration of the entire fifty days lay in the Jewish Omer Days—the seven weeks between Passover and Pentecost. But, again, while the Christian church took over the festival, it changed the spirit entirely. The Omer Days, at least the first part of them, were a kind of Lent in spirit, with marriages forbidden as well as haircuts and new clothes. These restrictions were relaxed on the thirty-third day, the Lag b'Omer, which was a kind of folk festival similar to the later European May Day.[1] Contrasted with this was the early Christian season of continuous celebration.

EASTER DAY
THE RESURRECTION OF OUR LORD

Easter Day is the "Queen of the Feasts" of the church year. Because our Lord rose from the dead on the first day of the

[1] Theodor H. Gaster, *Festivals of the Jewish Year, op. cit.,* p. 51ff.

week, every Sunday is an "Easter" and a commemoration of the resurrection, and the meeting of Christians for worship on Sunday appears to have begun on the Sunday after the resurrection.[2]

From the first, Easter has also been the day of all days for the celebration of the sacrament and the reception of Holy Communion, though to prevent unduly long services on Easter the interpretation of what constitutes an "Easter" communion was gradually broadened to include the Paschal season to Pentecost. In the sixteenth century the Protestant reformers preferred that there should be a communion every Sunday with communicants rather than that every communicant should appear on Easter Day.

The date of Easter may occur between March 22 and April 25, and it is the first Sunday after the first full moon after the vernal equinox. During the first three centuries there was a continuous and sharp difference of opinion about the date on which Easter ought to be kept each year. In the Eastern church, following the manner in which the Jews calculated the date of the Passover, the date of Easter was determined by the lunar month. Good Friday, they believed, was on the fourteenth day of the moon of the Hebrew month Nisan. Easter was then three days later, *regardless of the day of the week.* Good Friday might thus be on a Tuesday and Easter on Thursday! Those who supported this view were called *Quartodecimans* (the fourteenth day).

In the West, on the other hand, it was felt that Easter should always be observed on Sunday—the day of the resurrection; and that the crucifixion should always be commemorated on Friday. For western Christians it was the day of the *week* that was important; for the Eastern church, the day of the *month.*

[2] John 20:26. Cf. the hymn, "This Is the Day the Lord Hath Made."

The dispute was finally resolved at the Council of Nicaea (325 A.D.) and was a compromise in which both the moon and the day of the week were recognized. Easter was henceforth to be the first Sunday after the first full moon after the vernal equinox. This assured both parties that Easter would always recur at the time of the Passover, and that it would always occur on a Sunday. The council issued no canon on the subject, but its opinion was expressed in a letter from the emperor Constantine immediately following the council. There still remained, however, the difficulty of determining the vernal equinox, and various dates between March 18 and 25 were used, resulting in different Easters. In the fifth century, however, the Bishop of Alexandria, a city noted for its astronomical and mathematical research, was given the responsibility of determining the annual date of Easter, though the bishops there had been doing this unofficially much earlier.

In the third century, the Alexandrians had set the limits for Easter at March 22 and April 25, and it was essentially their system which was adopted by Dionysius Exiguus, a Scythian monk at Rome, who in 527 set up the Paschal Tables which have been used since. The chief error in the system was that it assumed a date of March 21 for the vernal equinox and assumed that the year was exactly 365¼ days long. Actually the solar year lacks a little over 11 minutes of this length, with the result that by 1582 the vernal equinox was on March 11 by the calendar. The correction, made under Gregory XIII in 1582 (and hence known as the Gregorian Calendar) dropped ten days from the calendar between October 5 and October 15. The change was made in most of western Europe then, but England and her colonies did not get around to it until 1752, by which time the necessary change amounted to twelve days instead of ten. The old (Julian) calendar is

still in use in some parts of the Eastern church. This accounts
for the fact that the date of Easter and the movable festivals
dependent upon it are sometimes different from the Western
dates. In the Gregorian Calendar the 11-minute-a-year error
of the old-style calendar is corrected by having only one
"century year" in four a leap year. Thus 1700, 1800 and 1900
were not leap years; 2000 will be. Since the accumulated error
amounts to three days in 399 years, this provision makes the
calendar as nearly approximate the actual solar year as possible.

The importance of all this to the church and its year is hard
to overestimate. The entire church year with the exception of
the six weeks from the First Sunday in Advent to the Epiphany,
and the fixed date festivals, depends upon the date of Easter.
And since Easter may vary more than a month, so may the
other dependent festivals. The six Sundays preceding Easter
are the Sundays in Lent; Ash Wednesday is 40 days (not
counting the Sundays) before Easter; Septuagesima is nine
weeks before Easter; the number of Sundays after the Epiphany
is determined by the Sundays between January 6 and Septuagesima. In the other direction, the Ascension is 40 days after
Easter; Pentecost, seven weeks after Easter; Trinity Sunday,
eight weeks after Easter; and the number of Sundays after
Pentecost or Trinity in any year is determined by the number
of Sundays between Trinity Sunday and the Sunday nearest
November 30.

The Epiphany and Pentecost or Trinity[3] seasons are like the
folds in an accordion. When Easter is early there may be only
one Sunday after the Epiphany, and 27 after Trinity or 28
after Pentecost. On the other hand, Easter can be so late that
there will be six Sundays after the Epiphany and only 22 after

[3] The ancient and present Roman use is to number the Sundays after Pentecost. The Lutheran and Anglicans have followed a later medieval practice of
numbering the Sundays after Trinity. The Tenth Sunday after Pentecost would
occur on the same Sunday as the Ninth Sunday after Trinity.

Trinity or 23 after Pentecost. The earliest and latest dates for the festivals dependent on Easter follow:

Septuagesima	January 18 to February 21
Ash Wednesday	February 4 to March 10
Ascension Day	April 30 to June 3
Pentecost	May 10 to June 13

It is not only the church which is concerned about our wandering Easter. Schools and colleges with "Easter" recesses find it difficult to synchronize instruction schedules with the religious holidays. The clothing trade must plan its spring offerings differently for a late Easter than for an early one. Florists and confectioners are adversely affected when Easter comes too close to Mother's Day or when Valentine's Day falls in Lent. In recent years there has been a move afoot to provide a fixed calendar in which Easter would always occur on Sunday, April 8, the exact midpoint of its current wanderings. In this calendar there would always be four Sundays after the Epiphany; Septuagesima would fall on February 5; Ash Wednesday on February 22; Ascension Day on May 16; Pentecost on May 26; Trinity Sunday on June 3. There would be 25 Sundays after Trinity or 26 after Pentecost; Advent Sunday would be December 3. The advantages of such a calendar, which has the support of many business groups as well as some churches, would be great. There would no longer be occasions when fixed date church festivals would collide with variable ones. The Annunciation, for instance, would always occur on the Monday after Passion Sunday, never in Holy Week as it often does at present. But more important would be the regularization of the year and its benefits for church school instruction, parish programs and events, etc. However, calendar reform is a long and slow process and it was 170 years before the western world adopted the present Gregorian system. The following table gives the dates of the festivals dependent upon our wandering Easter through 1979.

THE MOVEABLE FESTIVALS OF THE CHURCH YEAR
1955-1979

Year	1955	1956	1957	1958	1959
Sundays after Epiphany	4	3	5	3	2
Septuagesima	Feb. 6	Jan. 29	Feb. 17	Feb. 2	Jan. 25
Ash Wednesday	Feb. 23	Feb. 15	Mar. 6	Feb. 19	Feb. 11
Easter	Apr. 10	Apr. 1	Apr. 21	Apr. 6	Mar. 29
Ascension Day	May 19	May 10	May 30	May 15	May 7
Pentecost	May 29	May 20	June 9	May 25	May 17
Sundays after Trinity	24	26	23	25	26
Advent Sunday	Nov. 27	Dec. 2	Dec. 1	Nov. 30	Nov. 29

Year	1960	1961	1962	1963	1964
Sundays after Epiphany	5	3	6	4	2
Septuagesima	Feb. 14	Jan. 29	Feb. 18	Feb. 10	Jan. 26
Ash Wednesday	Mar. 2	Feb. 15	Mar. 7	Feb. 27	Feb. 12
Easter	Apr. 17	Apr. 2	Apr. 22	Apr. 14	Mar. 29
Ascension Day	May 26	May 11	May 31	May 23	May 7
Pentecost	June 5	May 21	June 10	June 2	May 17
Sundays after Trinity	23	26	23	24	26
Advent Sunday	Nov. 27	Dec. 3	Dec. 2	Dec. 1	Nov. 29

Year	1965	1966	1967	1968	1969
Sundays after Epiphany	5	4	2	5	3
Septuagesima	Feb. 14	Feb. 6	Jan. 22	Feb. 11	Feb. 2
Ash Wednesday	Mar. 3	Feb. 23	Feb. 8	Feb. 28	Feb. 19
Easter	Apr. 18	Apr. 10	Mar. 26	Apr. 14	Apr. 6
Ascension Day	May 27	May 19	May 4	May 23	May 15
Pentecost	June 6	May 29	May 14	June 2	May 25
Sundays after Trinity	23	24	27	24	25
Advent Sunday	Nov. 28	Nov. 27	Dec. 3	Dec. 1	Nov. 30

Year	1970	1971	1972	1973	1974
Sundays after Epiphany	2	4	3	6	4
Septuagesima	Jan. 25	Feb. 7	Jan. 30	Feb. 18	Feb. 10
Ash Wednesday	Feb. 11	Feb. 24	Feb. 16	Mar. 7	Feb. 27
Easter	Mar. 29	Apr. 11	Apr. 2	Apr. 22	Apr. 14
Ascension Day	May 7	May 20	May 11	May 31	May 23
Pentecost	May 17	May 30	May 21	June 10	June 2
Sundays after Trinity	26	24	26	23	24
Advent Sunday	Nov. 29	Nov. 28	Dec. 3	Dec. 2	Dec. 1

Year	1975	1976	1977	1978	1979
Sundays after Epiphany	2	5	4	2	5
Septuagesima	Jan. 26	Feb. 15	Feb. 6	Jan. 22	Feb. 11
Ash Wednesday	Feb. 12	Mar. 3	Feb. 23	Feb. 8	Feb. 28
Easter	Mar. 30	Apr. 18	Apr. 10	Mar. 26	Apr. 15
Ascension Day	May 8	May 27	May 19	May 4	May 24
Pentecost	May 18	June 6	May 29	May 14	June 3
Sundays after Trinity	26	23	24	27	24
Advent Sunday	Nov. 30	Nov. 28	Nov. 27	Dec. 3	Dec. 2

In the Roman Catholic church, what was once the first mass of Easter has been moved forward to Saturday with the result that the present Missal has propers for only one mass on Easter, as contrasted with three for Christmas. Both Lutheran and Episcopalian uses now have provisions for two services on Easter. The Anglican appointments[4] for the chief service include Col. 3:1-4 and John 20:1-10. If there are two communion services, at the earlier service 1 Cor. 5:6b-8 and Mark 16:1-8 may be used. The Lutheran use has retained the historic Easter propers, 1 Cor. 5:7-8 and Mark 16:1-7, for the later service; and appointed 1 Pet. 1:3-9 and John 20:1-18 for the early service if there be one. In addition, Luke 24:13-35 (the Walk to Emmaus) becomes the stated lesson for Easter afternoon or evening. The collect, in common use, is Gelasian in origin with some Gregorian editing. In the psalmody both the introit and gradual are marked by the reappearance of "alleluia" which has not been heard in the church since the Saturday before Septuagesima. Alleluia first entered the services of the Western church at Easter. Following the gradual in the Roman Catholic church, the medieval sequence, *Victimae paschali* (the authorship of which is ascribed to one Wipo in the eleventh century) is sung. This was the basis of Luther's Easter hymn, "Christ Jesus lay in death's strong bands." In Lutheran use, only the first line of the sequence is subjoined to the gradual.

Many popular customs have been associated with Easter— some of Christian and some of non-Christian origin. In some Eastern churches it is still customary for the priest to visit the homes of his parishioners on Easter Eve to bless the Easter food. Originally this was intended to check overindulgence in foods which had been banned during the long Lenten fast. In some medieval churches it was customary to "resurrect" alleluia from

[4] The United States, Irish and Scottish books.

the casket in which it had been entombed in the chancel at the beginning of Lent; or the figure of Christ or the cross or crucifix from the casket in which it had been laid on Good Friday. In England and Scotland egg-dyeing and egg-rolling at Easter were popular—the latter a custom inaugurated on the White House lawn in Washington by President Madison. Though a desultory affair until the presidency of Rutherford B. Hayes, it has been an annual event on Easter Monday for children under twelve, except for the years 1941-1953. In England, too, Easter marked the beginning of new terms both in the law courts and in the colleges and schools.

In many parts of Europe there were quite elaborate Easter plays which were staged on Easter Eve. A manuscript found at the famous monastery of St. Gall, Switzerland, and dating from the fourteenth century, details an Easter play in nine acts and 35 scenes covering the life of Christ from his baptism to the resurrection. In Holland, even more was added, including a prelude—the creation; the fall of Lucifer; the downfall of man; Balaam, Isaiah, and Virgil in search of a Saviour, etc.[5]

Easter week was anciently marked by daily services at which attendance was required of all those baptized on Easter Eve. These new members wore their white baptismal robes for these services, giving the name White Sunday (*Dominica in albis*) to the First Sunday after Easter. With the increasing emphasis on Lent during the Middle Ages, these services declined in importance, and, while the present Missal still contains masses for each day in Easter Week, the services are not well attended. In Lutheran use, many sixteenth-century church orders retained propers for Monday and Tuesday in Easter Week—a practice still retained by the Anglicans—though American Lutheran use retains propers for only a Monday service.

[5] Alt, *op. cit.*, pp. 386-9.

For An Early Service
    Propers: Introit—Luke 24:6a, 5b, 6b, 7a, 7c;
              Ps. 8:5b, 6a
              Collect—Gelasian
              Lesson—Isa. 25:6-9
              Epistle—1 Pet. 1:3-9
              Gradual—Ps. 118:24, 29; 1 Cor. 5:7b, 8a
              Gospel—John 20:1-18
              Creed—Nicene
              Proper Preface—Easter
              Color—White

For the Later Service
    Propers: Introit—Ps. 139:18b, 5b, 6, 1, 2a
              Collect—Gelasian
              Lesson—Dan. 3:8-25
              Epistle—1 Cor. 5:7-8 or 1 Cor. 15:20-26
              Gradual—Ps. 118:24, 29; 1 Cor. 5:7b, 8a
              Gospel—Mark 16:1-7
              Creed—Nicene
              Proper Preface—Easter
              Color—White

THE MONDAY AFTER EASTER

The only weekday in Easter week which is still assigned propers in Lutheran use is Monday. Formerly there were services each day, and after the Reformation many orders retained propers for Monday and Tuesday. The Lutheran and Anglican epistle is Acts 10:34-43; the Roman lesson begins with verse 37. The gospel, Luke 24:13-35, is the same in all three churches. In Lutheran use, the introit, collect and gradual of Easter are repeated.

Propers: Introit—(see Easter, later service)
　　　　Collect—(see Easter)
　　　　Lesson—Exod. 15:1-18
　　　　Epistle—Acts 10:34-43
　　　　Gradual—(see Easter)
　　　　Gospel—Luke 24:13-35
　　　　Creed—Nicene
　　　　Proper Preface—Easter
　　　　Color—White

QUASIMODO GENITI
THE FIRST SUNDAY AFTER EASTER

Other names for this Sunday are Low Sunday (the origin of this title is not known) and White Sunday. Those who had been baptized at Easter wore their white baptismal robes at the daily services which they attended in Easter week. The white robes were worn for the last time at mass on the octave of Easter (*octava paschae*, or *pascha clausum*). Later, when Easter baptisms ceased to be the custom, children dressed in white received their first communion on this Sunday. As early as the ninth century, it was customary in Germany to have confirmations on this Sunday, and this custom was continued in some Lutheran churches after the Reformation. It is certainly to be preferred to Palm Sunday, both historically and psychologically.

Like the Sundays in Lent, the Sundays after Easter took their popular titles from the opening words of their Latin introits, and these titles are continued in the modern Lutheran use, even though they have passed out of currency in the Roman Catholic church. *Quasimodo geniti* (as newborn babes) was also known popularly as "Thomas' Sunday" from the gospel for the day.

The Lutheran collect and gospel agree with the Roman use.

The epistle has two additional verses, ending at verse 12 instead of 10a. The Anglican collect is from the 1549 Prayer Book; the epistle agrees with the Lutheran use, and the gospel has been shortened to end at verse 23 instead of 31. The Lutheran introit has added Ps. 81:8 in the middle of the chant. The Lutheran gradual is a curious combination of the alleluia half of the gradual for Monday in Easter Week (Matt. 28:2b) as the first half of the chant, followed by John 20:26.

> *Propers:* Introit—1 Pet. 2:2a; Ps. 81:8, 1
> Collect—Gelasian
> Lesson—Gen. 32:22-30
> Epistle—1 John 5:4-12
> Gradual—Matt. 28:2b; John 20:26
> Gospel—John 20:19-31
> Creed—Nicene
> Proper Preface—Easter
> Color—White

MISERICORDIA DOMINI
THE SECOND SUNDAY AFTER EASTER

For some unknown reason, the title for this Sunday in most Lutheran service books reads Misericordia*s* Domini, an unknown Latin form. Since the first words of the Latin introit are *Misericordia Domini* (the goodness of the Lord), the only explanation seems to be that the title may have been a medieval colloquialism of German origin. Possibly only the first word "Misericordia" was used and the word "Sonntag" was added. In the course of time, and by elision, the "S" of Sonntag may have been subjoined to Misericordia. At least it is certain that both this Sunday and its predecessor were not always known by two-word titles, but were known as Quasimodo and Misericordia Sundays.[6] The new Lutheran *Service Book* restores the correct title.

This Sunday was also known as Shepherd Sunday. Both the epistle and gospel, as well as the second half of the gradual, refer to Christ as the Shepherd.

The Lutheran and Roman propers are identical for this Sunday. The Anglican collect is again from the 1549 English Prayer Book. The epistle has been lengthened by adding several verses at the beginning which belong to the next Sunday's epistle. The Anglican epistle begins at verse 19 instead of 21.

> *Propers:* Introit—Ps. 33:5b, 6a, 1
> Collect—Gelasian
> Lesson—Ezek. 34:11-16
> Epistle—1 Pet. 2:21b-25
> Gradual—Luke 24:35b; John 10:14
> Gospel—John 10:11-16
> Creed—Nicene
> Proper Preface—Easter
> Color—White

JUBILATE
THE THIRD SUNDAY AFTER EASTER

Once again the Sunday takes its name from the opening of the Latin introit *Jubilate Deo omnis terra*. The collect is from the oldest sacramentary, the Leonine. It contains, in its English translation, the verb "eschew" which, in some modern books such as the American Prayer Book, has been rendered "avoid." [7]

---

[6] The title *Misericordias Domini* is almost universal in Lutheran use both in Europe and America. The *Liturgie und Agende,* New York, 1855, uses the title at least five times, p. 227, *et al.* Current German Lutheran service books all use it.

[7] This removes some of the "flavor" of the collect. Eschew, pronounced "es-choo," can hardly be misinterpreted even if it is a rare English word.

The collect refers quite pointedly to the newly baptized Christians who joined the church at Easter.

The propers in Lutheran and Roman use are the same except for a slight difference in the ending of the epistle—verse 19 in the Missal, verse 20 in the *Service Book.* The Anglican epistle is shortened to end at verse 17 to provide for the beginning of last Sunday's epistle at verse 19. The conclusion of the gradual "and thus to enter into his glory" is not a quotation from St. Luke's Gospel and is probably an ancient liturgical text.

> *Propers:* Introit—Ps. 66:1, 2, 3
> Collect—Leonine
> Lesson—Isa. 40:25-31
> Epistle—1 Pet. 2:11-20
> Gradual—Ps. 111:9a; Luke 24:46b
> Gospel—John 16:16-22
> Creed—Nicene
> Proper Preface—Easter
> Color—White

CANTATE
THE FOURTH SUNDAY AFTER EASTER

This Sunday is named for the opening word of the Latin introit from Psalm 98: *Cantate Domino canticum novum* (O sing unto the Lord a new song). Because of its title it is often an occasion for special musical services in the Lutheran church.

The collect is Gelasian and the Lutheran translation is closer to the original Latin than Cranmer's version in the *Book of Common Prayer.* The epistle and gospel are common to all three Western liturgical churches. The introit and gradual are the same in Lutheran and Roman use, except for the addition in Lutheran books of verse 2a, "The Lord hath made known his salvation," to the introit.

How the gospels for the Third, Fourth and Fifth Sundays after Easter got scrambled is a mystery. From the Third Sunday after Easter through the Sunday after the Ascension (the Sixth Sunday after Easter), the church reads all of Jesus' farewell discourse from John 15:26 to 16:30, but it reads 15:26—16:4 on the Sixth Sunday; 16:5-15 on the Fourth; 16:16-23 on the Third; and 16:23-30 on the Fifth! In addition, the festivals of St. Mark (April 25) and SS. Philip and James (May 1) which usually fall in the Easter season, have as gospels John 15:1-11 and John 14:1-13, respectively. The gospel for Pentecost is John 14:23-31. All of these lessons are appropriate to the season of preparation for the Ascension and the coming of the Holy Ghost, but it would be surprising if this portion of St. John's Gospel had not once been read "in course."

> *Propers:* Introit—Ps. 98:1a, 2, 1b
> Collect—Gelasian
> Lesson—Isa. 29:9-14
> Epistle—Jas. 1:17-21
> Gradual—Ps. 118:16; Rom. 6:9
> Gospel—John 16:4b-15
> Creed—Nicene
> Proper Preface—Easter
> Color—White

ROGATE
THE FIFTH SUNDAY AFTER EASTER

Many Lutheran service books entitle this Sunday *Rogate* or *Vocem Jucunditatis,* the latter title coming from the first words of the Latin introit. The name *Rogate* comes from the three penitential "Rogation Days" (days of asking) which immediately follow this Sunday, and on which there were special litanies and prayers. Rogate Sunday, however, is a festival and not a penitential day, and the character of the Rogation Days should in no case be transferred to Sunday.

While the gospel lends itself to the rogation theme, the propers are older than the rogation days and their appropriateness is entirely coincidental. In Lutheran and Roman use the introit, collect, epistle and gospel are the same. The extrascriptural text of the opening verse of the Latin gradual has been replaced by the reformers with Luke 24:46b: "It behooved Christ to suffer and to rise from the dead and thus to enter into his glory." In Anglican use, the gospel is extended to end at verse 33.

> *Propers:* Introit—Isa. 48:29b; Ps. 66:1, 2
> Collect—Gelasian
> Lesson—Isa. 55:6-11
> Epistle—Jas. 1:22-27
> Gradual—Luke 24:46b; John 16:28
> Gospel—John 16:23b-30
> Creed—Nicene
> Proper Preface—Easter
> Color—White

THE ASCENSION OF OUR LORD

Originally the ascension was not celebrated as a separate event, but simply as part of the fifty-day period from Easter to Pentecost in which the entire redemption was commemorated. It appeared as a separate celebration in the fourth century in the Eastern church. The date—forty days after Easter —was determined by Scripture and one of its early names was *Quadragesima* (the fortieth day). Since this day was always a Thursday, Ascension Day was also known as Holy Thursday.[8]

---

[8] Maskell, *op. cit.,* vol. II, p. 242, cites an interesting fifteen century "simplified" creed: "he roose from deeth to lyue on the thridde day, and he stey to heuene on hooly thursday."

Until well into the Middle Ages, the festival was marked by
a procession. Sometimes, as at Antioch and Constantinople,
this was to a hill outside the city where services were held.
Such processions were popular in Germany and Gaul. In later
times these processions were replaced by the rogation procession on the three days preceding the Ascension. Another
custom still followed in the Roman and other churches was
the extinguishing of the paschal candle, which had been lighted
at each service since Easter, after the reading of the gospel for
the day. In some churches in the Middle Ages a figure of our
Lord was hoisted through an opening in the church roof.[9] New
beans were blessed at the Ascension Day mass.[10] This blessing
occurred just before the *per quem haec omnia* in the middle of
the canon of the mass.

In Protestant churches, Ascension Day and the Epiphany—
the two major festivals of the church year which occur on
weekdays (always the former, usually the latter)—are the forgotten festivals of the church. In the Roman Catholic church,
the Ascension is a holy day of obligation and the faithful must
attend church. In France, even under Napoleon, the Ascension
was one of the four days that survived as holidays. The others
were Christmas, the Assumption of the Virgin Mary (August
15) and All Saints' Day. All other holy days occurring on
weekdays were transferred to the following Sundays. This
happened to Ascension Day in Prussia, but elsewhere in the
Lutheran church it has been retained on its proper day.

The introit, collect, epistle, gradual and gospel are identical
in Lutheran and Roman use. The Lutheran *Service Book*

[9] Alt, *op. cit.,* p. 379, cites the Processionale von Bamberg, 1773, as a late
instance. Cf. also Kellner, *op. cit.,* p. 108. The medieval mind was greatly
impressed by such pageantry which would probably bring laughter from a
modern American congregation—especially if the rope stuck!

[10] L. Duchesne, *Christian Worship.* (5th Engl. ed.; London: S.P.C.K., 1949),
translated by M. L. McClure, p. 183. Grapes were similarly blessed on St.
Sixtus' Day (August 6).

provides an additional collect which, in another form, is used
by the Anglican church on the Sunday after the Ascension. It
was originally prepared for the 1549 Prayer Book and was
based on the antiphon sung at vespers on Ascension Day. In
the Lutheran version, it is addressed to Christ: "O King of
Glory, Lord of Hosts, who didst this day ascend in triumph far
above all heavens." It is one of the few stated collects addressed
to Christ. Another exception is the fact that the narrative of the
day is read in the epistle (as on Pentecost) rather than in the
gospel. American Episcopalians have as their gospel Luke
24:49-53, following the Ambrosian use of Milan and the
Eastern church, rather than the western gospel of Mark16:14-
20, which has been subject to heavy criticism by biblical
scholars as being a later appendage to St. Mark's Gospel.[11] The
Lutheran lectionaries of Eisenach and Thomasius also use the
Lukan account.

> *Propers:* Introit—Acts 1:11; Ps. 47:1
> Collects—(1) Gelasian; (2) Gregorian
> Lesson—2 Kings 2:9-15 or Gen. 5:21-24
> Epistle—Acts 1:1-11
> Gradual—Pss. 47:5; 68:18a
> Gospel—Mark 16:14-20
> Creed—Nicene
> Proper Preface—Ascension
> Color—White

EXAUDI
THE SUNDAY AFTER THE ASCENSION

The Missal calls this Sunday the Sunday within the octave
of the Ascension. Anciently it was called the Sixth Sunday

---

[11] The Revised Standard Version of the Bible sets this apart from the rest of
Mark to emphasize this. Most critics, however, concede that it dates from the
second century.

after Easter. This is its title in the Mozarabic (Spanish) and Gallican lectionaries of the eighth century.[12] And as late as 1763, Muhlenberg refers to it as "Exaudi. The Sixth Sunday after Easter." [13] It bears this title in Swedish use as well.[14] Actually, of course, the Paschal season extended from Easter to Pentecost, and this Sunday has many characteristics which tie it to the first five Sundays after Easter. The gospel belongs in the sequence with those of the Third, Fourth and Fifth Sundays; the gradual has the same structure which is peculiar to the Easter season, with its introductory alleluias, and the New Testament conclusion; and there is an absence of any reference to the Ascension as such. All of these point to its origin before the Ascension was set off as a separate festival. Like the other five Sundays after Easter, it continues the theme of the joy of the resurrection and the anticipation of the coming of the Holy Ghost on Pentecost. The Lutheran title, Exaudi, comes again from the opening word of the Latin introit *Exaudi, Domine, vocem meam* (Hear, O Lord).

The propers are all in Lutheran and Roman use. The Anglican collect is from the 1549 Prayer Book.

> *Propers:* Introit—Ps. 27:7a, 8, 9a, 1a
> Collect—Gelasian
> Lesson—Isa. 32:14-20
> Epistle—1 Pet. 4:7b-11
> Gradual—Ps. 47:8; John 14:18a, 28a
> Gospel—John 15:26—16:4a
> Creed—Nicene
> Proper Preface—Ascension
> Color—White

[12] Alt, *op. cit.,* pp. 144-5.
[13] *Journals, op. cit.,* vol. I, p. 629.
[14] Lindberg, *op. cit.,* p. 312, p. 531. The Lutheran Hymnary of the Evangelical Lutheran Church, in use by most American Lutherans of Norwegian ancestry, uses this title.

13.

PENTECOST AND ITS SEASON

The longest season of the church year, occupying half the year, is the time between Pentecost (May 10 to June 13) and the First Sunday in Advent (the Sunday nearest November 30).

Up until the seventh century, no special liturgical provisions were made for any of the ordinary Sundays of the year, the vast majority of which fall in the second half of the church year, the time after Pentecost. Instead there was a reservoir of common masses, any of which could be selected for any ordinary Sunday. The annual cycle of events connected with the life of our Lord, which began with Advent and concluded with Pentecost, contained a few Sundays after the Epiphany which were ordinary Sundays, but the bulk of them (between 23 and 28) followed Pentecost. For them there are no special services in the Leonine Sacramentary, and the Gelasian and Gregorian provide only common masses.

The very naming or numbering of these Sundays was not uniform. In Northern Europe and England, where the Festival of the Holy Trinity was popular, the medieval missals generally numbered the Sundays after Trinity, and this custom was carried into Lutheran use from the German missals, and into English use from the Sarum Missal. In some places there were attempts made to divide this long season into smaller cycles. The most popular dividing points were June 29, August 10 and September 29, which are the feasts of SS. Peter and Paul, St. Lawrence and St. Michael. The Sundays from Pentecost or

Trinity Sunday to SS. Peter and Paul were numbered in the usual way. Sundays between June 29 and August 10 were numbered as Sundays "after the Apostles"; those between August 10 and September 29, "after St. Lawrence";[1] and the remaining Sundays to Advent, "after St. Michael." Other dividing points were St. Cyprian (September 26) and the September Ember Days. These subdivisions of the time after Pentecost are as old as eighth-century France and as recent as the calendar of the Evangelische Kirche in Deutschland in 1947.[2]

In contrast, the Roman Catholic church continued to number its Sundays consecutively after Pentecost as they had been in primitive times, and after the liturgical reforms of Pius V in 1570 this system was officially adopted and all other customs suppressed. Since this was 53 years after the beginning of the Reformation, it is not surprising that the north European use of the Middle Ages is still reflected in Protestant calendars. In the Lutheran and Anglican enumeration of the Sundays, the number is always one less than the corresponding Sunday after Pentecost in the Roman Catholic church.

In the Eastern church, the Sundays of the second half of the church year are known by their respective gospels. From the Sunday after Pentecost to September 14 (Holy Cross Day) the gospels are from Matthew and the Sundays are known as the First, Second, Third, etc., Sunday after St. Matthew. From September 14 on, the gospels are from Luke and the Sundays are after St. Luke.

Since each Sunday from the Sunday after Trinity Sunday to

---

[1] St. Lawrence was accorded high honor in the medieval church, especially in Germany where many Lutheran churches bear his name, and his day was continued in many Lutheran calendars after the Reformation.

[2] After Trinity Sunday there may be up to four Sundays; then the "Sunday before the Apostles;" up to 13 Sundays after the Apostles; "Michael's Sunday;" up to seven Sundays after St. Michael's Day; the Last Sunday of the Church Year, and the Sunday of the Last Day (Judgment Sunday).

the Sunday before Advent is an ordinary Sunday and not a ranked festival, any day for which propers are provided takes precedence over it. Should, for instance, St. Matthew's Day (September 21) fall on a Sunday, its propers would displace those of the Sunday. The only item of the Sunday's propers which would be used would be the collect, which would be read as a second collect, immediately following the collect for St. Matthew's Day. The color of the day would be red instead of green.

While there may at one time have been some scheme used in the selection of particular lessons for particular Sundays during the time after Pentecost, and perhaps some circumstance calling forth a particular collect or introit or gradual, no such scheme is now discernible. This is due partly to the dislocations that have occurred with the passage of time. In Roman use the beginning of the season has been changed by the introduction of Corpus Christi (thirteenth century) on the Thursday after Trinity Sunday, with an octave; and the festival of the Sacred Heart of Jesus (eighteenth century) on the Friday after the octave of Corpus Christi. This has dislocated the historic gospels so that the gospel read in the Lutheran and Anglican churches is usually one week ahead of the Roman although the epistles are usually the same. To complicate matters still further, the Anglicans have shifted the historic collects so that they are one Sunday behind Lutheran and Roman churches! As a result of these dislocations, any "thematic harmony" which may exist among the propers for a particular day is likely to be a pure coincidence and in spite of, rather than because of, conscious effort.

The long season which begins with Pentecost, however, is used to apply to the Christian life the lessons of the first half of the year. We live in the age of the Spirit—an age which will continue until Christ comes again. This half of the church year is a "season of instruction and discipline complementary to, not continuous with, the seasons of historic commemoration, in which the implications of the historic revelation of Father, Son and Holy Spirit are studied and applied to the Church's inner life and outer witness." [3]

THE FESTIVAL OF PENTECOST. WHITSUNDAY

The word Pentecost means "fiftieth day." Like Pascha, the primitive Christian name for Easter, it was taken over into Christian use from the Jews. For them, Pentecost was the Feast of the Weeks, a celebration of the conclusion of the grain harvest. Bread made from the freshly-reaped grain was presented as an offering to God.[4] Later, and perhaps by the time of Christ, there came to be associated with the Jewish Pentecost the delivery of the Law to Moses on Mt. Sinai, and thus the "founding" of the Jewish "church." This later emphasis became more pronounced as "a conscious counterbalance to the Christian festival of Whitsunday." [5]

The title Whitsunday, which means White Sunday, and was the more popular title in English-speaking lands, comes from the white garments worn by those baptized at Pentecost, just as the Sunday after Easter was once called White Sunday for the same reason.

Pentecost was the conclusion of the church's first and earliest season, which began with Easter. St. Paul kept Pentecost with the Christians of Ephesus (Acts 20:6), and in the year 58 he spent Easter with the Philippian Christians, "not departing till the feast was over; and he then hastened on his journey and even sailed by Ephesus, in order to keep Pentecost in Jerusalem" (Acts 18:21; 20:6, 16). The continuity

[3] Shepherd, *op. cit.,* p. 186.
[4] Cf. Exod. 34:22; Lev. 23:15-17; Deut. 16:9-12.
[5] Gaster, *op. cit.,* p. 71.

of the season from Easter to Pentecost is indicated by St. Luke
who writes (Acts 2:1) "when the day of Pentecost was *fully*
come." Early Christians, quick to draw analogies, found in
Pentecost not only a thanksgiving for the fruits of the Spirit to
supplant the Jewish thanksgiving for the fruits of the earth, but
also the date of the founding of the Christian church to supplant the old dispensation symbolized by the delivery of the
Law to Moses.

In early centuries, Pentecost was the last call for baptisms
in the Western church. As at Easter, these ceremonies took
place on the vigil and were very similar. The services began on
Saturday afternoon and included many lessons, prayers, the
blessing of the font, the baptisms and, during the night, the
first mass of Pentecost. At first it seems to have been understood that baptism at Pentecost was reserved for those who,
through illness or some other equally valid reason, had been
prevented from receiving baptism at Easter. And, again as at
Easter, the time of these rites was pushed back to Saturday, and
in the modern Roman Catholic church they take place on Saturday morning. The Old Testament lessons and the blessing of
the font remain as relics of the ancient baptismal ceremonies.

Originally, since Pentecost itself brought to an end the high
season that began with Easter, it had no octave or prolonged
celebration. But by the time of the Gelasian Sacramentary,
there is provision for an octave of Pentecost. In the Gregorian
Sacramentary, there are services provided for Monday and
Tuesday after Pentecost as well. When the Ember Days were
fixed on the Wednesday, Friday and Saturday after Pentecost,
it was necessary only to provide a service for Thursday to give
each day of the week its own propers. Like Easter, Pentecost
has its own proper sequence, *Veni Sancte Spiritus,* which follows the gradual daily throughout the week.

In the Middle Ages, many local customs were associated

with Pentecost. In some churches, roses were strewn from the rafters to simulate the tongues of fire that appeared above the apostles' heads. In France, trumpets were sounded to recall the sound of the "rushing, mighty wind." In Italy, the day was called *pasqua rossa* from the red vestments. Most widespread, perhaps, was the use of a dove or pigeon to represent the Holy Ghost. Either a live dove or a carved one was let down by a rope from a hole in the church roof, or else set free in the church to fly off. A London lawyer named Lambarde wrote that he saw in 1536 "at St. Paul's a white pigeon let fly out of a hole in the roof of the great aisle." In 1330 the Canon of the Lincoln Cathedral paid sixpence to the clerk who led the dove. In 1609 it cost four shillings seven pence to replace the ropes in St. Patrick's Church, Dublin, so that the carved dove could be let down without danger to those below.

In England, where Monday was a holiday, there were morris dances and religious plays. The Whitsun Ale was famous. This was one of the "parish ales" which were parochial festivals featured by ale which was stronger than usual, and which was sold by the church wardens who used the proceeds for the repair of the church or for distribution to the poor.[6] These ales were of social importance in England in the Middle Ages and were usually held in the churchyard or a nearby barn. Colleges and universities used to brew their own ales and raise money by holding their own ales.[7] Such celebrating was not restricted to England and the (Lutheran) Saxon General Articles in 1557 inveighed against the excesses of the *"Pfingsttänze, Pfingstschiessens, Pfingstbiers."* But, while the English reformers tried to suppress these social activities, Luther could see no harm in them, and most Lutheran orders ignored them.

[6] The word "bridal" is derived from "bride ale," the celebration following a wedding.

[7] The prototype of the contemporary oyster supper of the women's auxiliary!

The New World was not without its own frolic, "Pinkster," named after the German word for Pentecost: *Pfingsten*. In colonial New York the most famous celebration was on Capitol Hill in Albany, which was known as Pinkster Hill. It was a slave frolic. "The Negroes kept up the fun for a week, dancing, eating gingerbread and drinking in honor of their legendary 'Old King Charley.' They used cast-off finery to bedeck themselves and consumed so much liquor that the bacchanalia had finally to be suppressed. On Long Island the festival was observed by whites as well as blacks; in parts of Pennsylvania and Maryland, usually by Negroes only." [8] The occasion as well as the title probably came from early Dutch settlers of New Amsterdam.

Muhlenberg was familiar with both the names for the festival (Pentecost and Whitsunday) and also with the keeping of Monday (which he calls "second Pentecost" in one place, and "Whitmonday" in others) with full services.[9]

The propers are common to both Lutheran and Roman use. The Anglican gospel begins at verse 15 instead of 23. Both chants, the introit and gradual, are worthy of note. The opening of the introit is from the first chapter of the Wisdom of Solomon, which is not canonical but is included in the Old Testament Apocrypha. The concluding verse of the gradual is a liturgical text which is not biblical at all, but the first lines of the sequence for Pentecost, *Veni Sancte Spiritus*.

> *Propers:* Introit—Wisd. of Sol. 1:7a; Ps. 68:3, 1
> Collect—Gelasian
> Lesson—Joel 2:28-32
> Epistle—Acts 2:1-11

[8] Herbert I. Priestley, *The Coming of the White Man* (New York: Macmillan, 1929), p. 342.
[9] *Journals, op. cit.,* vol. I, pp. 21, 279, 280, 390; II, p. 87.

Gradual—Ps. 104:30; *Veni Sancte Spiritus*
Gospel—John 14:23-31a
Creed—Nicene
Proper Preface—Pentecost
Color—Red

THE MONDAY IN WHITSUNWEEK

As at Christmas and Easter, Lutheran orders provide propers for the following day, though formerly they often provided for a three-day celebration. In America, even these one-day echoes of the festival are seldom observed today. The collect, epistle and gospel are the same in Lutheran and Roman use. In the Lutheran church, the introit and gradual for Pentecost are repeated on Monday. The Anglican epistle begins at verse 34 instead of 42.

Propers: Introit—same as Pentecost
Collect—Gelasian
Lesson—Isa. 57:15-21
Epistle—Acts 10:42-48a
Gradual—same as Pentecost
Gospel—John 3:16-21
Creed—Nicene
Proper Preface—Pentecost
Color—Red

THE FESTIVAL OF THE HOLY TRINITY

The early festivals of the Christian church are all commemorations of persons or events, either in the life of Christ or the life of the church. Not until comparatively lately were festivals instituted in honor of doctrines of the church. One of the earliest, and the one that has remained the most important, is the Festival of the Holy Trinity.

The early service books, when they have any title at all for this Sunday, call it the Sunday of the Octave of Pentecost, or the Sunday after Pentecost. Since it was a "vacant" Sunday, i.e., one without any assigned mass, many churches used on this day the office of the Holy Trinity prepared by Bishop Stephen of Liége (903-920) in the tenth century. This service was based on an earlier one in honor of the Trinity and recommended for Sunday use by Alcuin (d. 804) in cases where a priest did not have a complete missal. The so-called votive mass of the Holy Trinity, or mass of Alcuin, became the basis for the service of the Festival of the Holy Trinity.

Perhaps because it originated in northern Europe, the Festival of the Holy Trinity became very popular in the Low Countries, Germany, England and France, though originally it was opposed by the pope. Pope Alexander II (d. 1073) observed that no particular day should be set aside in honor of the Holy Trinity, since the Trinity was honored on every day in the church year. Despite such opposition, the festival was adopted by several monastic orders of considerable influence and a number of diocesan synods went on record in its favor. Finally in 1334, Pope John XXII ordered its general observance throughout the Western church.

Over most of northern Europe, the remaining Sundays of the church year were numbered after Trinity, though the manner of reading their titles leaves something to be desired.[10] In England, Trinity Sunday marks the beginning of one of the three-weeks' law court terms: Hilary, Easter, Trinity and Michaelmas. It is also, along with Michaelmas, Hilary and Easter, the beginning of a school term at Oxford.

The collect is Gregorian, though it goes back of the Gregorian Sacramentary to the votive mass of Alcuin. The epistle

[10] The First Sunday after Trinity, e.g., is an incomplete title. It should be the First Sunday after Trinity Sunday.

(which is used in both Lutheran and Roman services) is from Bishop Stephen's mass; the Anglicans have kept Rev. 4:1-11, which was the epistle for the octave of Pentecost. The gospel in use by both Lutherans and Anglicans is the old gospel for the octave of Pentecost; the Roman Catholic church uses Matt. 28:18-20. The introit and gradual chants are both based on the Old Testament Apocrypha—the former on Tob. 13; the latter on the Song of the Three Holy Children, which appears elsewhere in Lutheran use as a canticle and in the versicles at evening suffrages. The proper preface, used on Trinity Sunday and its octave, is Gelasian, and older than the remainder of the propers for the day.

> *Propers:* Introit—Liturgical text; Ps. 8:1a or
> Isa. 6:3; Rom. 11:36; Ps. 8:1a
> Collect—Gregorian
> Lesson—Isa. 6:1-8
> Epistle—Rom. 11:33-36
> Gradual—Song of Three Children 32, 34, 39
> Gospel—Matt. 28:18-20 or John 3:1-15
> Creed—Nicene
> Proper Preface—Trinity
> Color—White

THE FIRST SUNDAY AFTER TRINITY
(Second after Pentecost)

Since the Lutheran and Anglican churches number the Sundays after Trinity, and the Roman Catholic church numbers the Sundays after Pentecost, one would expect to find that the same propers used by Lutherans and Anglicans on the Fifth Sunday after Trinity are in Roman use on the Sixth Sunday after Pentecost and that the Fifth Sunday after Trinity and the Sixth Sunday after Pentecost would occur on the same Sunday.

In other words, it would be reasonable to expect all of Western liturgical Christianity to be using the same propers on the same calendar Sunday. Actually this never happens in the second half of the church year!

On the Fifth Sunday after Trinity, for instance, the Lutheran propers are: Introit: Psalm 27:7a, 9b, 1; Collect: *Deus, qui diligentibus* . . . ; Epistle: 1 Pet. 3:8-15; Gradual: Pss. 84:9, 8a; 31:1; Gospel: Luke 5:1-11. The Anglicans do not use introits and graduals, but their lessons are the same. The only departure is in the collect, *Da nobis, quaesumus Domine, ut et mundi cursus pacifice nobis tuo ordine dirigatur,* which the Lutherans used the Sunday before.

The Fifth Sunday after Trinity should be the Sixth Sunday after Pentecost, for which the Roman propers are: Introit: Ps. 28:8, 9, 1; Collect: *Deus virtutem, cujus est totum quod est optimum* . . . ; Epistle: Rom. 6:3-11; Gradual: Pss. 90:13, 1; 31:1; Gospel: Mark 8:1-9. The only item common is the closing verse (the alleluia) of the gradual: Ps. 31:1.

But, if we examine the Roman propers for the Fifth Sunday after Pentecost (one week earlier by the calendar than the Fifth Sunday after Trinity) we find: Introit: Ps. 27:7a, 9b, 1; Collect: *Deus, qui diligentibus te bona* . . . ; Epistle: 1 Pet. 3:8-15; Gradual: Pss. 84:9, 8a; 21:1; Gospel: Matt. 5:20-26. Here is almost complete agreement, except for the alleluia verse of the gradual and the gospel.

It is quite obvious that there have been a series of historical dislocations in the traditional propers as well as in the Sundays in the time after Pentecost. It is important to remember that the form of the Roman Missal was not set until 1570, which was 53 years after the Reformation, and that, with the exception of the collect, the Lutheran and Anglican series of propers exhibit a common tradition derived from the North European and English pre-Reformation missals—a use which differed in

certain respects from the Roman use which later became
standard.

The dislocation of the Sundays is due to the insertion of the
propers for Trinity Sunday into the older system, and the different manner in which the propers for the old First Sunday
after Pentecost were used. This Sunday was anciently a "vacant"
Sunday. It was the octave of Pentecost and had no propers of
its own. Later, however, the gospel which had been associated
with the Sunday after the old summer Ember Days (the Fourth
Sunday after Pentecost) was transferred to the First Sunday
after Pentecost. However, after the institution of the Feast of
the Holy Trinity, all of the propers which were associated with
the First Sunday after Pentecost fell into disuse, though they
remain in the Missal. In northern Europe, however, these
propers (using as the gospel the parable of the rich man and
Lazarus, from the Thursday after the Second Sunday in Lent)
were used on the First Sunday after Trinity Sunday. The
result was that the lessons used at Rome on the Second Sunday
after Pentecost were the same as those used in north Europe
on the Second Sunday after Trinity Sunday.

When the Fourth Sunday after Pentecost was reached, the
second dislocation—that of the epistles and gospels—occurred.
Since, in Roman use, the gospel for this Sunday, Luke 6:36-42,
had already been transferred to the First Sunday after Pentecost,
the Roman system simply moved the gospel for the Fifth Sunday after Pentecost up to the Fourth, and continued this dislocation throughout the remaining Sundays of the time after
Pentecost. In Northern Europe, the old gospel continued to
be used on the Fourth Sunday, and the ancient combinations of
epistles and gospels for the rest of the season remained.

One minor Lutheran dislocation is in the last verse (the
alleluia verse) of the gradual. Anciently, there were two
chants. One (the gradual) was between the Old Testament

lesson and the epistle; the other (the alleluia, or in Lent, the tract) was between the epistle and gospel. These were telescoped into one when the Old Testament lesson disappeared. The series of alleluia psalms from which Lutheran use is derived was slightly different from that adopted finally at Rome, so that, in general, the last verse of the Lutheran gradual is one Sunday ahead of the current Roman use.

A peculiar Anglican dislocation is the collect. For the first two Sundays after Trinity, there is agreement. But, on the Third Sunday after Trinity, the Anglicans use a collect which was peculiar to the Sarum Missal. It was not used at Rome, or in the north European missals from which Lutheran use is derived. On the Fourth Sunday after Trinity, the Protestant Episcopal church uses the collect read elsewhere on the Third Sunday, and continues this one Sunday dislocation throughout the Trinity season. This brings about the curious result that the same collect is read, for instance, on the Third Sunday after Pentecost in Roman churches; on the next Sunday, the Third Sunday after Trinity, in Lutheran churches; and on the following Sunday, the Fourth Sunday after Trinity, in Anglican churches!

Except for the Sunday dislocation, the epistles are common to Lutheran, Anglican and Roman use throughout the season, and the introits are common to Lutheran and Roman use.[11]

The propers for the First Sunday after Trinity in Lutheran use are the same as those in Roman use for the First Sunday after Pentecost, except for the gospel and the alleluia verse of the gradual. The gospel is that for the Thursday after the Second Sunday in Lent: the rich man and Lazarus. The final verse of the gradual is the same as that of the Second Sunday after Pentecost.

---

[11] Except at the end of the season, where the three churches use different methods in dealing with the variable number of Sundays.

Propers: Introit—Ps. 13:5, 6, 1
          Collect—Gelasian
          Lesson—Deut. 6:4-13
          Epistle—1 John 4:16b-21
          Gradual—Pss. 41:4, 1; 7:1
          Gospel—Luke 16:19-31
          Creed—Nicene
          Proper Preface—Trinity
          Color—White

THE SECOND SUNDAY AFTER TRINITY
(Third after Pentecost)

Propers: Introit—Ps. 18:18b, 19, 1, 2a
          Collect—Gelasian
          Lesson—Prov. 9:1-10
          Epistle—1 John 3:13-18
          Gradual—Pss. 120:1, 2; 7:17
          Gospel—Luke 14:15-24
          Creed—Nicene or Apostles'
          Proper Preface—none
          Color—Green

THE THIRD SUNDAY AFTER TRINITY
(Fourth after Pentecost)

Propers: Introit—Ps: 25:16, 18, 1, 2a
          Collect—Gregorian
          Lesson—Isa. 12:1-6
          Epistle—1 Pet. 5:6-11
          Gradual—Pss. 55:22a, 16, 18a; 18:1, 2a
          Gospel—Luke 15:1-10
          Creed—Nicene or Apostles'
          Proper Preface—none
          Color—Green

THE FOURTH SUNDAY AFTER TRINITY
(Fifth after Pentecost)

In the seventh century, the church observed summer Ember Days during the week preceding this Sunday, and the lessons for this Sunday were also assigned to the Ember Saturday which preceded it. When the Ember Days were moved to the week after Pentecost, the gospel was transferred at Rome to the First Sunday after Pentecost, but the epistle was left at this Sunday. The north European and Sarum missals kept the old lessons, and both Lutheran and Anglican churches have continued the older use.

> *Propers:* Introit—Ps. 27:1, 2, 3a
> Collect—Leonine
> Lesson—Num. 6:22-27
> Epistle—Rom. 8:18-23
> Gradual—Pss. 79:9b, 10a, 9a; 21:1
> Gospel—Luke 6:36-42
> Creed—Nicene or Apostles'
> Proper Preface—none
> Color—Green

THE FIFTH SUNDAY AFTER TRINITY
(Sixth after Pentecost)

In the early Middle Ages, the lessons of this Sunday were assigned to the Sunday before June 29, the Feast of SS. Peter and Paul, and both the epistle and the gospel reflect this tradition. As might be expected, both are concerned with St. Peter rather than with St. Paul.

> *Propers:* Introit—Ps. 27:7a, 9b, 1a
> Collect—Gelasian
> Lesson—Lam. 3:22-33

Epistle—1 Pet. 3:8-15a
Gradual—Pss. 84:9, 8a; 31:1
Gospel—Luke 5:1-11
Creed—Nicene or Apostles'
Proper Preface—none
Color—Green

THE SIXTH SUNDAY AFTER TRINITY
(Seventh after Pentecost)

With this Sunday the epistles begin a course of reading in the writings of St. Paul which continues up to the Last Sunday after Trinity. The epistles are from Romans (Sixth to Eighth Sundays), 1 Corinthians (Ninth to Eleventh), 2 Corinthians (Twelfth), Galatians (Thirteenth to Fifteenth), Ephesians (Sixteenth to Twenty-first, excepting the Eighteenth which is from 1 Corinthians), Philippians (Twenty-second and Twenty-third), Colossians (Twenty-fourth), and 1 Thessalonians (Twenty-fifth and Twenty-sixth). This is one of the few instances in which an ancient pattern can still be discerned in the propers. Other instances are the sequence of introit psalms and of alleluia psalm verses, both of which proceed through the psalter during the Trinity season with very few dislocations, as though there once were an in course chanting of the psalter.

Propers: Introit—Ps. 28:8, 9, 1
Collect—Gelasian
Lesson—Ruth 1:1-18
Epistle—Rom. 6:3-11
Gradual—Pss. 90:13, 1; 47:1
Gospel—Matt. 5:20-26
Creed—Nicene or Apostles'
Proper Preface—none
Color—Green

THE SEVENTH SUNDAY AFTER TRINITY
(Eighth after Pentecost)

The gospels for this Sunday and the next are thought to have had reference to the harvest, which was earlier in southern Europe than in America. The feeding of the four thousand is this Sunday's gospel; "by their fruits ye shall know them" is the Eighth Sunday's gospel.

Propers: Introit—Ps. 47:1, 3
Collect—Gelasian
Lesson—Isa. 62:6-12
Epistle—Rom. 6:19-23
Gradual—Pss. 34:11, 5; 59:1
Gospel—Mark 8:1-9
[end: "he sent them away."]
Creed—Nicene or Apostles'
Proper Preface—none
Color—Green

THE EIGHTH SUNDAY AFTER TRINITY
(Ninth after Pentecost)

Propers: Introit—Ps. 48:9, 10, 1
Collect—Leonine
Lesson—Jer. 23:16-29
Epistle—Rom. 8:12-17
Gradual—Pss. 31:2b, 1a; 1:6
Gospel—Matt. 7:15-21
Creed—Nicene or Apostles'
Proper Preface—none
Color—Green

THE NINTH SUNDAY AFTER TRINITY
(Tenth after Pentecost)

Both the epistle and the gospel for this Sunday present difficult problems. The epistle hardly makes sense when it begins, "Now these things were our examples," as it does in the Roman Missal and in most Lutheran books. The "things" which are our examples were read out, unfortunately, six months before on Septuagesima in the first five verses of 1 Cor. 10. The Anglicans and European Lutherans as well as the new *Service Book* begin today's epistle with 1 Cor. 10:1 and repeat the close of the Septuagesima epistle.

The gospel is the parable of the unjust steward, which is probably the most difficult of all Jesus' parables for both clergy and laity. On the other hand, the parable of the prodigal son, one of the clearest of Jesus' parables, is missing in the historic lectionary. It may once have been read on the Third Sunday after Trinity where it completes the trilogy of the lost sheep and the lost coin but, if so, it disappeared long ago. The American *Book of Common Prayer* (1928) and the Scottish book (1929) replaced the parable of the unjust steward with the parable of the prodigal son. The proposed English book (1928) suggested it as an alternate gospel for this Sunday, just as the Lutheran *Service Book* does.

> *Propers:* Introit—Ps. 54:4, 5, 1
> Collect—Leonine
> Lesson—Prov. 16:1-9
> Epistle—1 Cor. 10:1-13
> Gradual—Pss. 8:1; 78:1
> Gospel—Luke 16:1-9 or Luke 15:11-32
> Creed—Nicene or Apostles'
> Proper Preface—none
> Color—Green

THE TENTH SUNDAY AFTER TRINITY
(Eleventh after Pentecost)

The propers for this Sunday are believed to have been

selected with reference to August 10, near which this Sunday usually occurs. August 10 was the anniversary of the destruction of Jerusalem in the year 70. The gospel is our Lord's lament over the city. In parts of Germany, after the Reformation, women still wore mourning clothes to vespers and the hymn of Johann Heermann, *Du weinest für Jerusalem, Herr Jesu,* was sung.[12]

Propers: Introit—Ps. 55:16a, 17b, 18a, 19a, 22a, 1
Collect—Gelasian
Lesson—Jer. 7:1-11
Epistle—1 Cor. 12:1-11
Gradual—Pss. 17:8, 2; 59:1
Gospel—Luke 19:41-47a
Creed—Nicene or Apostles'
Proper Preface—none
Color—Green

THE ELEVENTH SUNDAY AFTER TRINITY
(Twelfth after Pentecost)

Propers: Introit—Ps. 68:5b, 6a, 35b, 1
Collect—Gelasian
Lesson—Dan. 9:15-19
Epistle—1 Cor. 15:1-10
Gradual—Pss. 28:7b, 1a, 2a; 65:1
Gospel—Luke 18:9-14
Creed—Nicene or Apostles'
Proper Preface—none
Color—Green

THE TWELFTH SUNDAY AFTER TRINITY
(Thirteenth after Pentecost)

Propers: Introit—Ps. 70:1, 2

[12] Alt, *op. cit.,* p. 531.

Collect—Leonine
Lesson—Isa. 29:17-21
Epistle—2 Cor. 3:4-9
Gradual—Pss. 34:1, 2; 81:1
Gospel—Mark 7:31-37
Creed—Nicene or Apostles'
Proper Preface—none
Color—Green

THE THIRTEENTH SUNDAY AFTER TRINITY
(Fourteenth after Pentecost)

Propers: Introit—Ps. 74:20a, 21a, 22a, 23a, 1
Collect—Leonine
Lesson—Zech. 7:4-10
Epistle—Gal. 3:16-22
Gradual—Pss. 74:20a, 21a, 22a, 23a; 88:1
Gospel—Luke 10:23-37
Creed—Nicene or Apostles'
Proper Preface—none
Color—Green

THE FOURTEENTH SUNDAY AFTER TRINITY
(Fifteenth after Pentecost)

Propers: Introit—Ps. 84:9, 10a, 1, 2a
Collect—Gelasian
Lesson—Prov. 4:10-23
Epistle—Gal. 5:16-24
Gradual—Pss. 118:8, 9; 90:1
Gospel—Luke 17:11-19
Creed—Nicene or Apostles'
Proper Preface—none
Color—Green

THE FIFTEENTH SUNDAY AFTER TRINITY
(Sixteenth after Pentecost)

Propers: Introit—Ps. 86:1a, 2b, 3, 4
Collect—Gelasian
Lesson—1 Kings 17:8-16
Epistle—Gal. 5:25—6:10
Gradual—Pss. 92:1, 2; 108:1
Gospel—Matt. 6:24-34
Creed—Nicene or Apostles'
Proper Preface—none
Color—Green

THE SIXTEENTH SUNDAY AFTER TRINITY
(Seventeenth after Pentecost)

Propers: Introit—Ps. 86:3, 5, 1
Collect—Gelasian
Lesson—Job 5:17-26
Epistle—Eph. 3:13-21
Gradual—Pss. 102:15, 16; 98:1a
Gospel—Luke 7:11-16
Creed—Nicene or Apostles'
Proper Preface—none
Color—Green

THE SEVENTEENTH SUNDAY AFTER TRINITY
(Eighteenth after Pentecost)

Propers: Introit—Ps. 119:137, 124a, 1
Collect—Gelasian
Lesson—Prov. 25:6-14
Epistle—Eph. 4:1-6
Gradual—Pss. 33:12, 6; 116:1
Gospel—Luke 14:1-11
Creed—Nicene or Apostles'

Proper Preface—none
Color—Green

THE EIGHTEENTH SUNDAY AFTER TRINITY
(Nineteenth after Pentecost)

This Sunday, which usually occurs after the fall Ember Days (the Wednesday, Friday and Saturday after September 14), was a "vacant" Sunday without propers. The introit, "let thy prophets be found faithful"; the epistle; the gradual, "I was glad when they said unto me, let us go into the house of the Lord"; and the gospel, are all appropriate to the ordinations which formerly took place at Embertide.

The introit, from the apocryphal book of Ecclesiasticus, is also the introit for the Roman votive mass for peace. The alleluia verse of the Lutheran gradual is taken from the tract for the Ember Saturday which preceded this Sunday.

> *Propers:* Introit—Ecclus. 36:16-17a; Ps. 122:1
> Collect—Gelasian
> Lesson—2 Chron. 1:7-12
> Epistle—1 Cor. 1:4-9
> Gradual—Pss. 122:1, 7; 117:1
> Gospel—Matt. 22:34-46
> Creed—Nicene or Apostles'
> Proper Preface—none
> Color—Green

THE NINETEENTH SUNDAY AFTER TRINITY
(Twentieth after Pentecost)

With this Sunday, the course reading of the Pauline epistles, which was interrupted on the Eighteenth Sunday after Trinity, is resumed. The introit has an extra-biblical text as an antiphon, and is the same introit used in a Roman votive mass "for any necessity."

Propers: Introit—Liturgical text; Ps. 78:1
Collect—Gelasian
Lesson—Gen. 28:10-17
Epistle—Eph. 4:17-28
Gradual—Pss. 141:2;118:16
Gospel—Matt. 9:1-8
Creed—Nicene or Apostles'
Proper Preface—none
Color—Green

THE TWENTIETH SUNDAY AFTER TRINITY
(Twenty-first after Pentecost)

Propers: Introit—Dan. 9:14b; Pss. 119:124; 48:1
Collect—Gelasian
Lesson—Prov. 2:1-9
Epistle—Eph. 5:15-21
Gradual—Pss. 145:15, 16; 105:1
Gospel—Matt. 22:1-14
Creed—Nicene or Apostles'
Proper Preface—none
Color—Green

THE TWENTY-FIRST SUNDAY AFTER TRINITY
(Twenty-second after Pentecost)

Propers: Introit—Rest of Esther 13:9-11a;
Ps. 119:1
Collect—Gelasian
Lesson—2 Sam. 7:18-29
Epistle—Eph. 6:10-17
Gradual—Pss. 90:1, 2; 125:1
Gospel—John 4:46b-53
Creed—Nicene or Apostles'

Proper Preface—none

Color—Green

THE TWENTY-SECOND SUNDAY AFTER TRINITY
(Twenty-third after Pentecost)

Propers: Introit—Ps. 130:3, 4, 1, 2a

Collect—Gelasian

Lesson—Prov. 3:11-20

Epistle—Phil. 1:3-11

Gradual—Pss. 133:1, 3b; 146:1b, 2a

Gospel—Matt. 18:21-35

Creed—Nicene or Apostles'

Proper Preface—none

Color—Green

THE TWENTY-THIRD SUNDAY AFTER TRINITY
(Twenty-fourth after Pentecost)

Propers: Introit—Jer. 29:11a, 12, 14b; Ps. 85:1

Collect—Gelasian

Lesson—Prov. 8:11-22

Epistle—Phil. 3:17-21

Gradual—Pss. 44:7, 8; 115:11

Gospel—Matt. 22:15-22

Creed—Nicene or Apostles'

Proper Preface—none

Color—Green

THE TWENTY-FOURTH SUNDAY AFTER TRINITY
(Twenty-fifth after Pentecost)

The closing Sundays of the church year are treated differently by the three Western liturgical churches. The Lutheran church provides propers for a full complement of twenty-seven Sundays after Trinity. The Anglican church provides propers for twenty-four Sundays after Trinity, and for the Sunday next before Advent (America) or the Twenty-fifth Sunday after Trinity (English). If there are 26 Sundays after Trinity, the propers for the Sixth Sunday after Epiphany are used; if 27, the propers for the Sixth Sunday after Epiphany are used on the Twenty-sixth Sunday and those for the Fifth Sunday after Epiphany are used on the Twenty-fifth.

In the Roman Catholic church, lessons and propers are provided for 24 Sundays after Pentecost. If there are 25 Sundays, the propers for the Third Sunday after Epiphany are used on the Twenty-fourth; if 26 Sundays, propers for the Fourth Sunday after Epiphany are used on the Twenty-fifth; if 27, those for the Fifth Sunday after Epiphany are used on the Twenty-sixth; if 28, the propers for the Sixth Sunday after Epiphany are used on the Twenty-seventh. In any case, the propers for the Twenty-fourth Sunday after Pentecost are used on the last Sunday of the church year.

The propers of these last Sundays often refer to the Second Coming. This emphasis on the Last Things—the Second Advent—probably goes back to the days when Advent was longer than its present four weeks, and began in some places as early as St. Martin's Day, November 11.

> *Propers:* Introit—Ps. 95:6, 7a, 1
> Collect—Gelasian
> Lesson—1 Kings 17:17-24
> Epistle—Col. 1:9-14
> Gradual—Pss. 1:1a, 2; 91:15a, 16
> Gospel—Matt. 9:18-26
> Creed—Nicene or Apostles'
> Proper Preface—none
> Color—Green

THE TWENTY-FIFTH SUNDAY AFTER TRINITY
(Twenty-sixth after Pentecost)

Propers: Introit—Ps. 31:9a, 15b, 17a, 1a[13]
　　　　　Collect—Gelasian
　　　　　Lesson—Job 14:1-6
　　　　　Epistle—1 Thess. 4:13-18
　　　　　Gradual—Ps. 91:2, 4b, 1
　　　　　Gospel—Matt. 24:15-28
　　　　　Creed—Nicene or Apostles'
　　　　　Proper Preface—none
　　　　　Color—Green

THE TWENTY-SIXTH SUNDAY AFTER TRINITY
(Twenty-seventh after Pentecost)

Propers: Introit—Ps. 54:1, 2, 5
　　　　　Collect—Swedish rite, 1639
　　　　　Lesson—Dan. 7:9-14
　　　　　Epistle—1 Thess. 5:1-11
　　　　　Gradual—Ps. 24:3, 4a, 5a; Isa. 43:1b
　　　　　Gospel—Matt. 25:31-46
　　　　　Creed—Nicene or Apostles'
　　　　　Proper Preface—none
　　　　　Color—Green

THE LAST SUNDAY AFTER TRINITY
(The Last Sunday after Pentecost)

The propers are peculiarly Lutheran except for the collect, which is that of the Twenty-third Sunday after Trinity repeated. The gospel, the parable of the ten virgins, recalls St. Catherine's Day (November 25), which occurred near this Sunday each year and for which this was the gospel.

---

[13] This is the introit for Friday after Passion Sunday in the Roman Missal.

In some sections of the Lutheran church, the last Sunday after Trinity has been observed as *Todtenfest,* a service of commemoration of the faithful departed.[14] In other places, this service was held on St. Sylvester's Day, December 31. In the former case, it was at the end of the church year; in the latter, at the end of the civil year. The ecclesiastically preferred dates were, of course, November 1 and 2, All Saints' Day and All Souls' Day, respectively, but the reformers felt that at least the latter of these two festivals could hardly be kept without continuing certain unevangelical practices associated with it in medieval times.

> *Propers:* Introit—Rev. 22:13; 21:3; Ps. 24:7
> Collect—Gelasian
> Lesson—Isa. 35:3-10
> Epistle—2 Pet. 3:8-14
> Gradual—John 8:12b; Rev. 22:17, 20b
> Gospel—Matt. 25:1-13
> Creed—Nicene or Apostles'
> Proper Preface—none
> Color—Green

[14] E.g., Prussian Agende of 1806. Cf. Alt, *op. cit.,* p. 110

14.

SAINTS' DAYS AND HOLY DAYS

In addition to the fifty-day period from Easter to Pentecost, the most ancient festivals of the church were the commemorations of its martyrs on the day of their death or, as the early church phrased it, their "birthday" to eternity. Some of those who died in New Testament times are noted in its pages: the Holy Innocents, St. James, and St. Stephen. As the church spread and persecutions increased in extent and severity, each congregation kept a record of those of its number who had met death for their faith. Their names and the dates of their martyrdom were recorded. Sometimes, in larger Christian communities, the bishop appointed notaries to secure and keep correct records of all martyrdoms. Their names were entered in the calendar of the church on the date of their death and their memory was noted each year on the proper anniversary. Similar rolls of bishops were kept, and there are extant fragments of some of these rolls (*depositio martyrum,* and *depositio episcoporum*) dating from the fourth century.

At first only martyrs were admitted to the calendars. One of the first after New Testament times was Polycarp, Bishop of Smyrna, who was martyred in 156. He was also one of the earliest martyrs to gain general recognition. Martyrs had to have more than local reputation to secure more than local commemoration. Later, after Constantine, when the true (or more often, "alleged") body of the martyr was moved from its original resting place to a more fitting tomb in a church, his

name and the date, either of his martyrdom or of the translation of his relics, was entered in the calendar.

Names of saints who were not martyrs began to appear in
calendars from the beginning of the sixth century. Some were
prominent as bishops, or confessors, or doctors. Two of the
earliest, in whose honor churches were dedicated at Rome about
500, were St. Sylvester and St. Martin of Tours. Later, the
anniversaries of the dedication of important churches found
their way into the calendar, too.

The cycle of observances in honor of the Virgin Mary, which
has now become so extensive that, in popular devotions in the
Roman Catholic church, it threatens to overshadow the cycle
of our Lord, began with the Annunciation and the Presentation,
both of which were originally included in the calendar as
festivals of our Lord, and not of the Virgin Mary. The Annunciation was called *Festum conceptionis Domini*. Only in
later centuries in the Roman Catholic church did the title "the
Presentation of our Lord" give way to "the Purification of the
Blessed Virgin Mary."

Until the eighth century each congregation retained some
autonomy in its calendar, though by then calendars had become
more regional than purely local. But in that century, the
Roman calendar along with the Roman service books became
the standard of Western Christianity. In the process there had
to be many adaptations, and saints commemorated in Gallican
and Mozarabic calendars came gradually to be accepted in the
official Roman list. The process of canonization, however, was
difficult to centralize. Bishops continued to bring forward local
saints despite papal efforts to restrict them, and it was not until
well after the Reformation, in 1634, that Pope Urban VIII was
able to confine the process of including new saints in the
calendar to the action of the papal curia at Rome.

In the meantime the calendar had gotten well out of hand and there were literally thousands of saints, with not a free day left in the year. Not all of them received ecumenical veneration, but each of them received some commemoration somewhere. In the sixteenth century there was demand for the reform of the calendar, both in ecclesiastical circles where the problems of protocol caused by the frequent coincidence of special days had necessitated a highly complicated system of ranking festivals,[1] but also in secular circles where overly-frequent holidays interfered unduly with the developing commercial economy.

It was into such a situation that the Protestant reformers stepped in 1517. The Lutheran church orders generally retained only those festivals and the commemoration of those saints noted in or founded upon Holy Scripture. But there was no uniformity, either of principle or practice, and some Lutheran orders retained St. Lawrence, St. Sylvester, the Invention and Exaltation of the Holy Cross, Corpus Christi, the Assumption of the Virgin Mary, and rejected St. Mary Magdalene, St. Barnabas and St. Timothy, though none of the former and all of the latter are "scriptural." In Hamburg (1539) St. Mary Magdalene, Holy Innocents, St. Lawrence and St. Ansgar (Hamburg's first archbishop and the apostle to the Northlands) remained in the calendar.[2] Hesse (1532) kept St. Peter's Chains (Lammas) and the Decollation (Beheading) of St. John the Baptist. Mark-Brandenburg (1540) kept Corpus Christi, St. Mary Magdalene, St. Lawrence, the Assumption and the Nativity of the Virgin Mary, St. Martin and St. Catherine.[3] Nassau (1536) kept Corpus Christi and St. Lawrence, as well

---

[1] Some of the systems used in medieval times for ranking festivals were ingenious, i.e., eight copes, three copes, nine psalms, three lessons, nine lessons, high, semi-high!

[2] A. L. Richter, *Die evangelischen Kirchenordnungen des sechszehnten Jahrhunderts* (Leipzig: Ernst Julius Gunther, 1871, 2 vols.), I, p. 319.

[3] *Ibid.*, pp. 332-3.

as the Assumption and the Nativity of the Virgin Mary.[4] The
calendar of the Church of Sweden was exceptionally full, including among many others, both festivals of the Holy Cross,
St. Sylvester, St. Lucy, St. Peter's Chair, St. Barnabas, St. Bernard,
St. Augustine, St. Francis of Assisi, St. Cecilia, St. Gregory, St.
Ambrose, St. Catherine, St. Martin and half a dozen Scandinavian saints.[5]

Not all of these festivals, however, were retained with their
pre-Reformation propers and emphasis. The reformers tried
to make them evangelical. In 1527 Luther himself wrote some
Festpostils or meditations for St. Mary Magdalene, St. Lawrence,
the Assumption and Nativity of the Virgin Mary, St. Catherine,
the Decollation of St. John the Baptist, the Invention and the
Exaltation of the Holy Cross, St. Barbara, St. Nicholas and St.
Anne, even though he had objected to some of these festivals
at other times.[6] Some of these festivals were of great popularity
in northern Europe. The reformers could not ignore the Assumption (August 15), yet they could not accept it with its
medieval connotations. The Brandenburg-Nürnberg Order
(1533) retained it with the note that, though the day had no
scriptural basis, yet for the sake of the common people the day
was to be kept in the churches and the story of the Visitation
was to be read. In Schwabisch-Halle (1543) it is called "The
Departure of Mary." It was specifically banned in Osnabrück
(1543).

Another troublesome festival because of its popularity was
Corpus Christi, accompanied as it was by grand processions in
Germany. Nassau (1536) permitted it but without the procession or the exposition of the Blessed Sacrament. But it was
not until 1572 that Brandenburg, which had retained Corpus

[4] *Ibid.*, p. 278.
[5] Lindberg, *op. cit.*, p. 408ff.
[6] His objections to the Festivals of the Holy Cross were because of the
processions. Cf. Luther's *Works*, Erlangen ed., vol. XV, p. 359f; XVI, p. 459f.

Christi in its 1540 order, felt it possible to abandon it in favor of Maundy Thursday as an evangelical festival of the sacrament.

The tendency, however, in the Lutheran church which, following the Reformation, had to live through the Thirty Years' War, Pietism, and Rationalism, was to accept the calendars of the most narrow group of church orders, and in general, the principle of a scriptural basis. This latter point had best not be pressed, however, since Reformation Day, All Saints' Day and even Trinity Sunday would be difficult to defend, and St. Mary Magdalene, St. Barnabas, St. Timothy, the Decollation of St. John the Baptist and possibly other festivals would be difficult to exclude. For these there is not only good scriptural foundation, but also considerable more information than we possess about St. Matthias or St. Simon or St. Jude.

The Anglican reformers, who adopted the same general principle, were also guilty of some inconsistencies. St. Barnabas was accepted, but the Visitation and, most surprising of all, the Transfiguration, were excluded. But, since they were followed by the entire Church of England, the Anglican reformers were able to achieve a greater degree of uniformity. Each Lutheran church order applied only to the political area of the then-fragmented German nation for which it was prepared.

In ranking the festivals they retained, both Lutherans and Anglicans discarded the complicated classifications of the medieval church. The Lutherans divided the festivals into greater and lesser. The Anglicans, in theory, reduced all festivals to equal rank. In practice, however, they set up a table of precedence which resulted in a division on the whole analogous to the Lutheran division. The chief variations are that in Lutheran calendars the Circumcision, Transfiguration and Reformation Day rank as greater festivals; while in the Anglican calendar the first of these is a minor, the second (though omitted in 1549) is now a minor, and the third does not appear.

The Anglicans, on the other hand, rank as major festivals the days of Easter Week and of Whitsun Week. These differences are quite minor. Needless to add, the Calvinists and Zwinglians took a very dim view of saints' days and holydays, though Calvin himself appears to have held a more historic point of view.

While it may be that the reformers took the only practical course at the time, both the Lutheran and Anglican calendars could be improved. Of some of the Apostles, for instance, while they are certainly "scriptural," we know nothing at all other than very uncertain legends of quite late date. We know more, and of a more reliable nature, about St. Augustine, St. Ambrose, St. Lawrence, St. Francis and St. Martin, for instance, than we know of St. Bartholomew. Another factor which ought to carry some weight is the antiquity of the festival in the church and its ecumenical observance. The introduction of some festivals now in the Lutheran calendar is much later than many festivals which are excluded. St. Barnabas is "scriptural" and his day appears in Eastern calendars from the fifth century. This is 800 years before the introduction of the Visitation. A final weakness is that the calendar as now constituted gives the impression that after the apostolic age nothing of importance occurred until October 31, 1517. There is nothing in it to remind the people of the great souls who lived the faith and sometimes died for it, either during the fifteen centuries before the Reformation or the four centuries since. Few bits of evidence could better play into the hands of those who charge the Protestant church with being a new church, founded in the sixteenth century!

The Anglican church has met this difficulty by adding to its "red letter days" (the official saints' days and holydays) a group of "black letter days." The American Prayer Book has provided a set of propers for "A Saint's Day," leaving the selection of the saint to the parish priest. Had the Lutheran church continued to operate on the basis of the ancient church, its calendar might include commemorations of the deaths of Luther and perhaps in America, Muhlenberg. Whether they should be designated as "saints" or not is another matter, and both would be first to protest. But it is at least open to question whether the title of "saint" should be restricted only to those who are mentioned in Scripture, or only to those who have been properly certified by the Roman Curia.

The lives of the saints continually remind us of the great host of witnesses in the faith who have gone before us and who, we believe, are still our examples and our encouragement in the Christian life. They are also a reminder of the continuing existence of the body of Christ—the Church—and of the fact that whether it be militant and on earth or triumphant and in the joy of its Lord in heaven, it is one, holy, catholic church, timeless and composed of God's people of every age.

Even though America was not inhabited by Christians during the Middle Ages, the names of saints were carried to the New World by the explorers, and the priests who sailed with their expeditions. Jacques Cartier dropped anchor at Gaspé and discovered Canada on August 10, 1535, St. Lawrence's Day, and the name of the saint became attached to both the river and the bay. In 1602, the Spanish explorer Viscaino sailed up the coast of California and it is possible to date his voyage by the names he left behind: San Diego (November 12), Santa Catalina (November 25), San Pedro (November 28), Santa Barbara (December 4), Conception (December 8) and the Santa Lucia Mountains (December 13). He had on board some Discalced Carmelites. Dom Domingo Teran and the friar Damian Massanet discovered a Texas river on May 13, 1691, the day of St. Anthony of Padua, and it became the San Antonio River, later giving its name to the city on its banks.

Among American cities, Los Angeles (El Pueblo de la Reina de los Angeles de la Porciuncula is the full name!), St. Louis, San Francisco, Santa Fe, Corpus Christi, Sacramento, San Diego, San Antonio, St. Paul, San José, St. Petersburg, San Bernardino, St. Joseph and San Angelo reflect the hold the saints had on early settlers. Nor are all the saints' names in areas that were once Spanish or French. St. George, St. James, St. Albans and St. Johnsville are all in New York; St. Davids and St. Martins in Pennsylvania; St. Asaph and St. Brides in Virginia; St. Andrews, St. George, St. Matthews, and St. Stephen in South Carolina; St. Albans in Vermont. Lutheran settlers named St. Ansgar and St. Olaf in Iowa. Americans are not without reminders of saints on the land, even though their names may not appear in Protestant calendars.

ST. ANDREW, APOSTLE — NOVEMBER 30

St. Andrew was the brother of St. Peter. He was one of the first disciples (John 1:37ff.) and the first Christian "missionary" in bringing his brother to our Lord. After the resurrection nothing certain is known of his labors, though a tradition as old as the second century states that he traveled to Scythia (modern Roumania) and to Epirus and Greece. There he is supposed to have met his martyrdom on November 30, being crucified on a X-shaped (saltire) cross. He was buried in Patras. In 357 his relics, as well as those of St. Luke, were removed to Constantinople. The church there claimed St. Andrew as its first bishop. His is the only festival of an apostle occurring on the exact day of his supposed martyrdom. The day appears in calendars of the Eastern church from the fourth century, and in the West in all calendars from the sixth century. His X-shaped cross appears as one of the transverse members of crosses atop the spires of Eastern Orthodox churches throughout the world, and in the flags of Scotland and

England. In iconography, he is usually represented either holding a cross saltire or leaning upon one.

St. Andrew's Day is of liturgical importance since it determines the date of the beginning of the church year which is the Sunday nearest or upon St. Andrew's Day, November 30. It is also the national day of Scotland. Some of the relics of the saint are alleged to have been translated from the East to St. Andrew's, Scotland. Scotsmen all over the world who are members of the St. Andrew's Society gather on November 30 to wear the heather and eat the haggis in commemoration of the patron saint of their native land.

> *Propers:* Introit—Common of Apostles
> Collect—*Book of Common Prayer,* 1549
> Lesson—Ezek. 3:16-21
> Epistle—Rom. 10:10-18
> Gradual—Common of Apostles
> Gospel—Matt. 4:18-22
> Creed—Nicene
> Proper Preface—All Saints
> Color—Red

ST. THOMAS, APOSTLE — DECEMBER 21

St. Thomas is most famous for his skepticism which has earned the phrase "doubting Thomas" a place in idiomatic English. He was unwilling to believe in the resurrection until he had seen and touched Jesus after the resurrection. (John 20:27ff.). Earlier, Thomas' skeptical remark, "Lord, we know not whither thou goest, and how can we know the way," had brought forth Jesus' comforting answer, "I am the way, the truth and the life."

Quasimodo Geniti (the First Sunday after Easter) is popularly known, because of its gospel, as "Thomas Sunday." The name Thomas means "twin" and Didymus was a synonym for it.

Of Thomas' activities after Pentecost we know nothing surely. He is said by tradition to have labored in Persia and in India, though his connection with a group of Christians on the Malabar Coast who call themselves "Thomas Christians" is generally doubted, and they are believed to be of Nestorian origin. Where or when he met his death is not known, but one of the greatest of the early basilicas (fourth century) was the Church of St. Thomas in Edessa, Syria, where his body was said to have been buried. His day appears in early Syrian and Greek calendars on October 6, and was generally observed in the East from the sixth century. In the West his day was not generally accepted until the ninth century, and then on the present date, December 21. The reason for the particular date is not known. Since the Sundays in Advent are all major festivals, St. Thomas' Day is observed only on a weekday.

> *Propers:* Introit—Common of Apostles
> Collect—*Book of Common Prayer,* 1549
> Lesson—Judg. 6:36-40
> Epistle—Eph. 1:3-6
> Gradual—Common of Apostles
> Gospel—John 20:24-29
> Creed—Nicene
> Proper Preface—All Saints
> Color—Red

THE CONVERSION OF ST. PAUL — JANUARY 25

This is the only festival retained by the reformers which is not a double of the first or second class in the Roman calendar. This is partly because, before the Reformation, this day was a holy day of obligation in much of Germany and in all of England. When and how it became so is not known. The principal observance of St. Paul was on June 29, when both he and St. Peter were commemorated. Since the propers of that day deal with St. Peter, the medieval church had an additional commemoration of St. Paul alone on June 30. This resulted in a peculiar situation in the Anglican calendar. The English reformers eliminated the June 30 commemoration and then proceeded to limit June 29 to St. Peter alone! The Lutheran reformers retained both St. Peter and St. Paul on June 29.

There may have been an ancient festival connected with St. Paul at or near Sexagesima, of which the epistle, the long catalogue of his trials, may be a remnant. But the event commemorated on January 25 was one of the most momentous in the history of the apostolic church. It is recounted three times in Acts—once in the narrative (Acts 9:1-22), once by St. Paul in his defence on the stairs (Acts 22:3-21) and again by the Apostle before King Agrippa (Acts 26:9-20).

The first appearance of the day in the calendar seems to have been in Gaul in the sixth century. It was accepted at Rome in the tenth century, and became a holy day of obligation in the archdiocese of Cologne in 1308. In iconography, St. Paul is represented as resting upon a sword; holding one or two swords; or sometimes with three springs of water at his feet—springs which were supposed to have gushed forth from the three spots where his head bounded after his decapitation!

Even though it was a Tuesday in frontier America, Muhlenberg observed the day in 1743 with a service at Providence.[7]

> *Propers:* Introit—Common of Apostles
> Collect—Composite
> Lesson—Jer. 1:4-10
> Epistle—Acts 9:1-22

[7] *Journals, op. cit.,* vol. I, p. 87.

Gradual—Common of Apostles
Gospel—Matt. 19:27-29
Creed—Nicene
Proper Preface—All Saints
Color—Red

THE PRESENTATION OF OUR LORD — FEBRUARY 2

This day is popularly known as Candlemas, and in the Roman Catholic church as the Purification of the Blessed Virgin Mary. In the ancient church it was sometimes called St. Simeon's Day, or *Occursus Domini* after the Eastern title, *Hypapante,* which means "the meeting" (i.e., of Simeon and the infant Jesus). The incident is related in Luke 2:22ff. Mary went to the Temple for the fulfilment of the Levitical requirement for the "churching of women" after childbirth. According to Lev. 12:2-8, a mother remained unclean for 40 days after the birth of a son (80 days for a daughter), after which she had to come to the Temple and be ritually readmitted to public worship.

The date of February 2 was determined by the interval of 40 days after December 25. In the primitive Eastern church, when the birth of our Lord was still celebrated on January 6, the Presentation was on February 14. In fourth-century Jerusalem it was called *Quadragesima de Epiphania* and is still observed on the February date in Armenia. In 542 the Emperor Justinian ordered the observance on February 2 throughout the church. At first this festival was one of our Lord and not, as it later became, one of the Virgin Mary. And it remains in the Lutheran church a feast of our Lord.

In medieval Rome an added ceremony was the blessing and distribution of candles with a procession, from which the title Candlemas comes. The procession goes back to Pope Sergius I (seventh century) and the blessing of the candles to the eleventh century. As in other cases, this was the sublimation of a previously existing pagan festival in Rome. There was a pagan feast of lights in which torchbearers repeated Ceres' search for Proserpine. In contemporary Roman use, the people proceed in double file, each holding a candle in the outer hand. During the procession, the church bell is rung. In many countries the candles are returned to the church, but in England they are retained by the people, who use them at sick calls, clinical communions and at the bedside of dying persons. Other candles blessed at Candlemas are not distributed at all, but are kept for church use during the ensuing year.[8]

Popular superstition has long associated this day with the weather. In medieval times, if February 2 brought fair weather, the winter would be long and crops bad. If Candlemas were a bad day, the winter was over and crops would be good. In many parts of rural America this superstition survives, though with the less churchly title of Groundhog Day. In medieval England, Candlemas was one of the four quarterly "sabbaths of witches." The others were Roodmas (May 1), Lammas (August 1), and All Hallow's Eve (the eve of November 1).

> *Propers:* Introit—Ps. 48:9, 10, 1
> Collect—Gregorian
> Lesson—Hag. 2:6-9
> Epistle—1 Cor. 1:26-31
> Gradual—Ps. 48:9, 10a; Isa. 11:12a, 12c
> Gospel—Luke 2:22-32
> Creed—Nicene

[8] Bruce Marshall, *The World, the Flesh and Father Smith, op. cit.,* pp. 17-18: "Mrs. Flanagan was at the door to meet him, in a fine state of sweat and nerves and holding a monster lighted candle in her hand, because she knew that the priest would be carrying the Host. . . . In the bedroom . . . Mrs. Flanagan had already placed a crucifix, two lighted candles, and a glass of water on the bedtable, because she always kept these things handy, since she didn't want to run any risks when the Lord called upon her to kick the bucket herself."

Proper Preface—Christmas
Color—White

ST. MATTHIAS, APOSTLE — FEBRUARY 24

Of St. Matthias, selected to fill the place of Judas, nothing is known either before or after the event related in Acts 1:15ff. One tradition places his ministry in Judaea; another in Ethiopia. That there must indeed have been a paucity even of legend is indicated when a ninth-century writer, Autpert, Abbot of Monte Cassino, states that nothing is known of St. Matthias! His day dates from early in the eleventh century, one of the last of the apostles' days, but the reason for the choice of February 24 is not known. In iconography St. Matthias is represented holding a halbert; leaning on a sword; holding a sword by the point; with a stone in his hand; with a book and scimitar.

Propers: Introit—Common of Apostles
Collect—Composite
Lesson—Isa. 66:1-2
Epistle—Acts 1:15-26
Gradual—Common of Apostles
Gospel—Matt. 11:25-30
Creed—Nicene
Proper Preface—All Saints
Color—Red

THE ANNUNCIATION — MARCH 25

Like the Presentation, this festival was originally a festival of our Lord, rather than of the Virgin Mary. One of its early titles was *Festum conceptionis Domini,* the conception of our Lord. Like the Presentation, too, its date is determined by the date of Christmas. With the setting of December 25 as the Nativity, March 25 became the date for the Annunciation. In England the popular name for the festival is Lady Day.

The event commemorated is recorded in Luke 1:26-38. Verse 28, "Hail thou that art highly favored, the Lord is with thee," is the basis for the Ave Maria. The Annunciation appears to have been observed in the East as early as the fourth century, and certainly in the fifth. In the West the first mention of the festival is in the seventh century. In the Mozarabic calendar in Spain, the Annunciation, as one of the events preceding the birth of Christ, was celebrated in Advent on December 18, rather than nine months before his birth.

March 25 was anciently believed to have been the date on which the world was created, and some old calendars carry the notation *Natale Mundi* opposite the date. The day was "New Year's Day" in England down to the eighteenth century. In primitive Christian times our Lord's death was thought to have occurred on March 25. This made the days of the Annunciation and the Crucifixion in the church year coincide, with disastrous results for the former. Today, with a movable Easter, the Annunciation still falls in Lent most of the time, and often in Holy Week, in which case it must await observance until after Easter. It would appear as if the old Mozarabic date were preferable.

> *Propers:* Introit—Ps. 45:12b, 14, 15a, 1a
> Collect—Gregorian
> Lesson—Mic. 5:2-4
> Epistle—Phil 4:4-9
> Gradual—Ps. 45:2b, 7a; Isa. 7:14b
> Gospel—Luke 1:26-38
> Creed—Nicene
> Proper Preface—Christmas
> Color—White

ST. MARK, EVANGELIST — APRIL 25

The saint commemorated on this day is John Mark, companion of St. Peter (1 Pet. 5:13), of St. Paul and St. Barnabas (Acts 12:25, 13:5, 15:37f.; Col. 4:10) and the traditional author of the second Gospel. He is generally credited with having been the founder of the church in Egypt where he is said to have been martyred at Alexandria in the year 64 in an attempt to stop the worship of Serapis. His remains were translated from Alexandria to Venice in 829 and are supposed to rest under the high altar of St. Mark's Cathedral.

His festival is thought to be earlier than the eighth century in the East. It appears in most Western calendars from the ninth century. In the Roman calendar, however, it does not appear until the twelfth century, which is surprisingly late, possibly because his relics were at Venice rather than at Rome.

In England, on St. Mark's Eve, it was popularly believed that, if one watched from the church porch, one could see the shades of all who would be buried in the churchyard during the ensuing year file slowly and silently past. In Scotland, the day was known as "Flitting Day," a sort of community moving day on which people who had notified their landlords on Candlemas of their intention to do so, moved to new homes.

Long before April 25 became St. Mark's day in the Western church, the date had been marked by a procession known as the *litania major.* This replaced an old Roman procession, the *robigalia,* which took place on the same day (vii Kalends Mai) and was designed to avert mildew (*robigo*) from the wheat. The major litany was well established on April 25 in sixth century Rome. The service appears in the present Roman Missal.

St. Mark is represented by a lion, or with a lion at his side.

Propers: Introit—Common of Evangelists
Collect—*Book of Common Prayer,* 1549
Lesson—Isa. 55:1-5
Epistle—Eph. 4:7-16
Gradual—Common of Evangelists
Gospel—John 15:1-11
Creed—Nicene
Proper Preface—All Saints
Color—Red

ST. PHILIP AND ST. JAMES, APOSTLES — MAY 1

Of these two apostles we know little more than their names. Philip, who came from the village of Bethsaida in Galilee, was one of the first of Jesus' disciples. A fellow-townsman of Andrew and Peter, he was responsible for bringing Nathanael into the number of the twelve (John 1:43ff.). Tradition states that he lived at Hierapolis, a town in Phrygia, where he also died, leaving two spinster daughters who lived to a great age and were also buried at Hierapolis. He is not to be confused with the Philip who, along with Stephen, was one of the first deacons of the church in Jerusalem (Acts 6:5) and who preached in Samaria (Acts 8:5ff.) and to the Ethiopian eunuch (Acts 8:26ff.). In iconography, Philip the Apostle is represented with a basket in hand; with two loaves and a cross; crucified head down; with a tall cross and book.

We know even less about St. James the Less. The three Jameses who were prominent in the apostolic church have been much confused in Christian tradition. James, the son of Zebedee, the brother of the disciple John, was the only apostle whose death is recorded in Holy Scripture (Acts 12:2). His day is July 25. A second James, described as the brother of the Lord, was the first bishop of the church in Jerusalem, over which he presided for thirty years (Acts 12:17; 15:13), suf-

fering martyrdom in 62. According to tradition, he was beaten
to death. Perhaps unconsciously, or possibly because of later
Roman doctrine which denied the existence of any brothers of
Jesus, this James, Bishop of Jerusalem, was confused in the
church's tradition with James the Less, the son of Alphaeus and
one of the twelve. The result is that we have no certain information about the discipleship, labors or death of James the
Less. In addition, there has never been any day in the calendar
in honor of James, Bishop of Jerusalem, who is certainly en-
titled to such honor on any basis, scriptural or otherwise. In
iconography, this confusion has been carried over into Christian
art, and James the Less is represented with a fuller's club (the
instrument with which James of Jerusalem was killed), or as a
child with a palm branch, or with a saw in hand.

The association of the two apostles with each other and with
May 1 is entirely due to the dedication of the Church of the
Apostles at Rome on May 1, under Pope John III (561-574),
at which time the alleged relics of the two disciples were transferred to the new basilica. After 561 the day appears in Western calendars and in the Gelasian Sacramentary.

In medieval times, May Eve, or Roodmas, was one of the four
sabbaths of witches. In north Europe there was an ancient
pagan festival on May 1, and the day was marked by sacrifices
to appease the devil. Before it became St. Philip's and St. James'
Day, May 1 was observed in north Europe as St. Walpurgis'
Day. Walpurgis died in 780 as Abbess of the Monastery of
Heidenheim, Germany. After her death, her relics were translated to Eichstatt, and the cave where she was buried became
a place of pilgrimage, and she came to be regarded as a pro-
tectress against hexerei and magic arts. Goethe has preserved
her memory in the Walpurgis Night dance in *Faust,* which
Mendelssohn later set to music.

Propers: Introit—Common of Apostles

Collect—*Book of Common Prayer,* 1549

Lesson—Mal. 3:16-18

Epistle—Eph. 2:19-22

Gradual—Common of Apostles

Gospel—John 14:1-13a

Creed—Nicene

Proper Preface—All Saints

Color—Red

THE NATIVITY OF ST. JOHN, THE BAPTIST
JUNE 24

One of the earliest festivals of the saints to gain universal recognition was that of St. John the Baptist, cousin and forerunner of our Lord. In the Eastern church he ranks next only to Christ and the Virgin Mary. In the West his day was important as early as the time of St. Augustine, who has left seven sermons for the occasion. His day appears in calendars from the fifth century, and in the Leonine and all subsequent Roman sacramentaries. The date, which once was close to the Epiphany, was finally set after Christmas was accepted as December 25. Since John was six months older than Jesus (Luke 1:36), the date of his birth was June 24. It is worthy of note as the exception to the rule, that while all other saints are remembered on the date of their death, John the Baptist is commemorated on the date of his birth. To remedy this, a second festival of John the Baptist appeared from the time of the Gelasian Sacramentary, on August 29, called the Decollation, or Beheading, of John the Baptist.

After John's death, his disciples took his body and buried it (Matt. 14:12; Mark 6:29). The head, which had been presented to Salome, was, of course, missing. The rest of his body was translated to Alexandria where a church was erected in his honor in the fourth century. His head supposedly was brought to Constantinople in the fourth century under the emperor Theodosius, and a fragment of it was reputedly taken to Amiens in the thirteenth century.

In iconography he is represented by a lamb on a book; in a tunic of camel's hair; with a lamb and a cross; by a head on a platter.

In the Middle Ages this festival was one of holy obligation and a holiday from all servile work. Not only did the faithful have to attend church, but their own parish churches. This was true of large areas of Germany including Cologne, Treves, Hannover, Hildesheim, Osnabrück, Bavaria, Württemburg, and Baden. Muhlenberg held services on this day in 1747.[9]

Popularly in England the day was known as Midsummer's Day, which explains the title of Shakespeare's play, *A Midsummer Night's Dream*. On its eve, as on the Eve of St. Mark, it was believed that the shades of all those who would die during the coming year could be seen approaching the church door.

> Propers: Introit—Isa. 40:3, 5a; Ps. 92:1
>   Collect—Lüneberg Church Order, 1564
>   Lesson—Mal. 4:4-6
>   Epistle—1 John 1:1-4
>   Gradual—Luke 1:76; John 1:15, 29b
>   Gospel—Luke 1:57-80
>   Creed—Nicene
>   Proper Preface—All Saints
>   Color—Red

ST. PETER AND ST. PAUL, APOSTLES — JUNE 29

In contrast to most of the apostles, a great deal is known

Journals, op. cit., vol. I, p. 156.

about the two leaders of the early church who are commemorated together on this day, though we have only traditions about their deaths and the traditions do not agree. According to one, both St. Peter and St. Paul suffered martyrdom at Rome on the same day, June 29 in the year 67, by order of the Emperor Nero. According to another, they both met death on June 29, but in different years. Still another tradition says that both were martyred, but that the date was February 22 in the year 68. In some early Gallican calendars this date appears as that of the burial (*depositio*) of SS. Peter and Paul. The day continues, in the present Roman calendar, as the Festival of St. Peter's Chair at Rome. Actually, we do not know if either or both of the apostles died at Rome, or when either of them died.

What is known, however, is that in 258, during the persecution of Valerian, this festival was instituted on June 29. "The commemoration was held at a catacomb on the Appian Way, where now stands the basilica of St. Sebastian, and recent excavations have brought to light devoted invocations of the Roman Christians to their greatest saints scribbled upon the walls of the room where they assembled for their anniversary banquets in honor of the apostles." [10] It is possible, too, that the apostles may have been buried in a catacomb, perhaps this one, and that June 29 marks the date of the translation of their relics to their later and known resting places: St. Peter's in the cathedral on the Vatican Hill, and St. Paul's in his church on the Ostian Way. It is probable that the distance between these two churches was responsible for separating the commemorations and making June 29 one of St. Peter (there is nothing in the propers about St. Paul), and setting June 30 as a commemoration of St. Paul.

This day was one of the dividing dates of the long season

[10] Shepherd, *op. cit.,* p. 244.

after Pentecost in the early Middle Ages. The Sundays were grouped after Easter until the Sunday "before the Apostles," and then "after the Apostles" until St. Lawrence's Day (August 10).

> *Propers:* Introit—Common of Apostles
> Collect—*Book of Common Prayer*, 1549
> Lesson—Jer. 26:12-16 or Isa. 22:20-23
> Epistle—Acts 12:1-11 or Gal. 1:11-20
> Gradual—Common of Apostles
> Gospel—Matt. 16:13-19
> Creed—Nicene
> Proper Preface—All Saints
> Color—Red

THE VISITATION — JULY 2

This day was originally one of the lesser festivals of the Virgin Mary, and of comparatively late origin (thirteenth century). But because of its scriptural basis (Luke 1:39ff.) and the Magnificat (Luke 1:46ff.) which it evoked, it was retained by the Lutheran reformers, though not by the Anglicans. It is the only festival of the Virgin retained in Lutheran calendars generally (a few retained the Assumption on August 15 and the Nativity on September 8) which was not originally a feast of our Lord. It is not in the calendar of the Eastern church.

The promotion of the festival was largely due to the Franciscans in the thirteenth and fourteenth centuries and finally, in 1441, the Council of Basel authorized the festival and granted indulgences to those present at divine services on the day. As was true of the Annunciation, a good argument could be made for placing the commemoration of the visit of Mary to Elizabeth in Advent.

Propers: Introit—Same as for the Annunciation
Collect—Strassburg Church Order, 1524
Lesson—Judg. 13:2-7 or Song of Sol. 2:8-14
Epistle—1 Pet. 3:1-5a
Gradual—Same as for the Annunciation
Gospel—Luke 1:39-47
Creed—Nicene
Proper Preface—Christmas
Color—White

ST. JAMES THE ELDER, APOSTLE — JULY 25

The James commemorated on this day (cf. SS. Philip and James, May 1) is the son of Zebedee, brother of St. John, and the first apostle-martyr. He is the only apostle whose martyrdom is recorded in the New Testament (Acts 12:2). A native of Galilee, he was an active leader of the early church, active enough to incur the enmity of Herod Agrippa I. His martyrdom occurred near Easter in the year 43 or 44. In early Eastern calendars his day is near Easter (April 12 in the Coptic Church; in Syria, April 30). The reason for the selection of July 25 as his day is not known, but it may have been the date of a translation of his relics. In the sixth century, his remains were said to be still in Jerusalem, though there was an ancient tradition that St. James had preached in Spain. In the ninth century his relics were said to be in Compostela, Spain, and his appearance in Western calendars generally dates from that century. In some English calendars, he is quaintly titled St. James the More, to distinguish him from St. James the Less (May 1). In iconography James is represented as a pilgrim with a staff; with staff and wallet; with staff and a book.

Propers: Introit—Common of Apostles
Collect—Leonine (SS. Simon and Jude)

Lesson—1 Kings 19:9-18
   [begin: "And Elijah came thither . . ."]
Epistle—1 Cor. 4:9-15
Gradual—Common of Apostles
Gospel—Matt. 20:20-28
Creed—Nicene
Proper Preface—All Saints
Color—Red

THE TRANSFIGURATION OF OUR LORD — AUGUST 6

This scriptural festival (Matt. 17:1-9; Mark 9:2-10; Luke 9:28-36) has been a major festival in the Eastern church since the fourth century, and has been observed in the West since the ninth century. In 1456 John Hunyadi and the great Franciscan preacher, Juan Capistrano, won a great victory over the Turks in a crusade at Belgrade. Capistrano died there of the plague. In token of thanksgiving for the victory, Pope Callixtus III in 1457 assigned the Feast of the Transfiguration its present date of August 6 and made it an ecumenical festival. The date had previously been kept in the East.

Because of its scriptural basis, it was retained in the Lutheran calendar, though omitted by the English reformers from the 1549 Prayer Book. In 1561 it was included as a black letter day. It first became a red letter day in the 1892 American Prayer Book, and since has been taken into all Anglican calendars.

In Lutheran use, however, there has been a difference of dates. The Church of Sweden has continued August 6, but many German orders of the sixteenth and seventeenth centuries adopted the Transfiguration propers for the Sixth Sunday after the Epiphany. A fixed date festival in August gets scant attention except when it falls on a Sunday, and there was Roman precedent in transferring the Transfiguration propers (cf. the

Second Sunday in Lent). The American *Common Service Book,* following the precedent established by the *Church Book,* set the Transfiguration propers for the *last* Sunday after the Epiphany in every year except when there was only one Sunday after the Epiphany. There is some merit in this arrangement. The transfiguration was a spectacular manifestation of our Lord, and it was after this incident that Jesus set his face towards Jerusalem. It is, however, a departure from the practice of ecumenical Christianity to neglect the date of August 6 for the festival. The Lutheran *Service Book* restores the propers to August 6, and repeats them for the Sixth Sunday after the Epiphany. In years when there are not six Sundays after the Epiphany, the Transfiguration propers *may* be used on the last Sunday after the Epiphany, except when there is only one Sunday after the Epiphany.

> *Propers:* Introit—Pss. 77:18b; 84:1, 2a
> Collect—Roman, fifteenth century
> Lesson—Exod. 34:29-35
> Epistle—2 Pet. 1:16-21
> Gradual—Pss. 45:2a; 110:1; 96:2, 3
> Gospel—Matt. 17:1-9
> Creed—Nicene
> Proper Preface—Epiphany
> Color—White

ST. BARTHOLOMEW, APOSTLE — AUGUST 24

Again we have an apostle of whom nothing is certainly known. That he is the same person as Nathanael (John 1:45f.) is only conjecture. Various traditions have him laboring in Arabia, on the shores of the Bosphorus, in India and Persia. The place, date and manner of his death are not known. His festival seems to have originated in the Eastern church, and appears in Western calendars after the eighth century. The reason for the date of August 24 is unknown, but it is believed to have been the date of the translation of his relics.

The day is best remembered for the ruthless slaughter of the Huguenots in 1572. Plotted by Catherine de Medici, the Dukes of Anjou and Nevers, and Henry of Guise, the massacre continued until September 17 in Paris, and to October 3 elsewhere. More than 50,000 Protestants died, though the plotters (as in the case of Herod and the Holy Innocents) failed to kill their chief objective, Admiral Coligny. Impressed by this latter-day "crusade," Pope Gregory XIII had a special medal struck in honor of the massacre of St. Bartholomew's Eve.

In iconography, St. Bartholomew is represented with a knife and book; or with knife in hand, and the devil under foot.

> *Propers:* Introit—Common of Apostles
> Collect—Composite
> Lesson—Prov. 3:1-7
> Epistle—1 Cor. 12:27-31a
> Gradual—Common of Apostles
> Gospel—Luke 22:24-30
> Creed—Nicene
> Proper Preface—All Saints
> Color—Red

ST. MATTHEW, APOSTLE, EVANGELIST
SEPTEMBER 21

About St. Matthew we know little beyond Matt. 9:9ff. He is believed to have been the author of the first Gospel which bears his name, and, according to tradition, he labored in Ethiopia after the resurrection. His day is of Eastern origin, and in the Greek, Russian, Syrian and Armenian calendars is on November 16. The Western date of September 21 which appears in the ninth century, is believed to be the date of a translation of his relics.

In iconography he is represented as leaning on a short sword; with an angel holding an inkstand; an angel with a human face; with a halbert, book and inkhorn.

> *Propers:* Introit—Common of Apostles
> Collect—*Book of Common Prayer,* 1549
> Lesson—Ezek. 1:4-14 or Prov. 30:7-9
> Epistle—Eph. 4:7-16
> Gradual—Common of Apostles
> Gospel—Matt. 9:9-13
> Creed—Nicene
> Proper Preface—All Saints
> Color—Red

ST. MICHAEL AND ALL ANGELS — SEPTEMBER 29

The popular name for this festival is Michaelmas. In many ancient calendars it was one of the dividing points of the Trinity season. It was the only festival of the angels retained by the reformers. (The Roman calendar provides for St. Gabriel on March 18, St. Raphael on October 24, and the Guardian Angels on October 2.) Possibly because of this, the reformers added to the title "and All Angels." [11]

The festival had its origin in the dedication of a church to St. Michael and was the only festival of that type to find a place in early Roman calendars. The church was on the Via Salaria, about six miles north of Rome, and was dedicated to St. Michael on September 29. In the present Missal the day still bears the title, *Dedicationis S. Michaëlis Archangeli.* The

---

[11] The title All Angels appears to have been used first for this day in the church order of the Bohemian Brethren in 1524. Cf. Richter, *op. cit.,* vol. II, p. 485.

day appears in the Leonine and all subsequent sacramentaries. It was especially popular in northern Europe and England. In France it was adopted at the Council of Tours (858). In England by the eleventh century it had a vigil and a three-day preparatory fast. In Germany it was adopted at the Council of Mainz in 813, and later became a holy day of obligation at Cologne, Hildesheim, Osnabrück and elsewhere.

In England, Michaelmas marked the beginning of the fall term in the law courts, as well as the fall scholastic terms at Oxford and Cambridge. The popular name for the aster was Michaelmas daisy, and a custom almost as popular as America's turkey on Thanksgiving was goose on Michaelmas in medieval England.

> *Propers:* Introit—Ps. 103:20, 21, 1
> Collect—Gregorian
> Lesson—2 Kings 6:8-17
> Epistle—Rev. 12:7-12
> Gradual—Pss. 103:20; 103:1; 91:11
> Gospel—Matt. 18:1-10
> Creed—Nicene
> Proper Preface—All Saints
> Color—White

ST. LUKE, EVANGELIST — OCTOBER 18

There is surprisingly little reliable information about St. Luke. According to an early tradition he is supposed to have been a native of Antioch and an early convert to Christianity. He is referred to as "the beloved physician" (Col. 4:14) and was a companion of St. Paul. He may have been left in charge of the church at Philippi between St. Paul's first and second visits, and he is believed to have been with the apostle during his two imprisonments at Caesarea and at Rome. Another tradition holds that St. Luke was one of the seventy commissioned by our Lord, and that he was an artist. He is the evangelist credited with the third Gospel and with its sequel, the Book of Acts.

After the apostolic period covered in the New Testament, St. Luke is said to have preached in Bithynia and to have lived to the age of 84. There is no information about his death, though another old tradition places his death and burial at Thebes. His relics were supposedly discovered and translated along with those of St. Andrew (*q.v.*) to Constantinople and placed in the Church of the Apostles on March 3, 357. His festival appears first in the West in the eighth century, although it may have been observed earlier in the East. However, the date, October 18, is the same in all calendars and may be the traditional date of his death. In iconography, St. Luke is represented by an ox; with an ox lying near; with paints and palette; as a physician.

> *Propers:* Introit—Common of Evangelists
> Collect—Composite
> Lesson—Isa. 35:5-8
> Epistle—2 Tim. 4:5-11
> Gradual—Common of Evangelists
> Gospel—Luke 10:1-9
> Creed—Nicene
> Proper Preface—All Saints
> Color—Red

ST. SIMON AND ST. JUDE, APOSTLES
OCTOBER 28

Of these two disciples nothing is known beyond the fact that they are paired together in the lists in Luke 4:14-16 and in Acts 1:13. One tradition has Simon laboring for the gospel in

Egypt, Cyrene and Mauritania; and Jude is said to have married and raised a family, but to have accompanied Simon. A stronger tradition states that the two apostles went together to Persia, spent thirteen years there in missionary labors, and were martyred in the city of Suanir at the same time. The date of their martyrdom, according to this tradition, was July 1. A third tradition identifies Jude with Thaddaeus, and places his labors and those of Simon in Armenia. Their festival dates from the ninth century in the West, although the reason for the date of October 28 is not known.

In iconography, St. Simon is represented with a fish in hand; with a fish on the leaves of an open book; with an oar; sawn through longitudinally. St. Jude is represented with a boat in hand; with a boat hook in hand; carrying loaves or fish.

> *Propers:* Introit—Common of Apostles
> Collect—*Book of Common Prayer,* 1549
> Lesson—Jer. 26:16-19
> Epistle—1 Pet. 1:3-9
> Gradual—Common of Apostles
> Gospel—John 15:17-25
> Creed—Nicene
> Proper Preface—All Saints
> Color—Red

REFORMATION DAY — OCTOBER 31

This is the only festival in the Lutheran calendar which is peculiar to the Lutheran church. It is the anniversary of All Hallow's Eve 1517, when Luther, then an Augustinian and professor at the University of Wittenberg, nailed his 95 statements on the sale of indulgences to the door of the church. He knew they would be seen by many, for All Saints' Day was a holy day of obligation and all the faithful would be in church the next morning. He did not know that he was initiating the Protestant Reformation. The division of Christendom, later forced by the pope's bull of excommunication, was the farthest thing from the mind of Luther in 1517. Then he had an almost naive optimism about the possibility of reforming the abuses of the Western church from within. Even after the division, Luther maintained the place of evangelical Christianity in the holy catholic church and would probably have objected to a Festival of the Reformation, both because it would give the Lutheran church the appearance of newness, and because it would not have contributed to the reconciliation of Christendom.[12]

There was some celebration of the Reformation in the sixteenth century, but only six of the several hundred Lutheran church orders make any provision for it, and not all of them are agreed, either on the nature of the observance or on the date. Bugenhagen, in the orders for Brunswick (1528), Hamburg (1529) and Lübeck (1531), provides for a Reformation festival. The next appearance is in 1563 (Elector Joachim) and 1568 (Pomerania). The Pomeranian Order set the festival for St. Martin's Day, in memory of Luther's birth.[13] Some orders selected Trinity Sunday, thus following the birth of the Christian church on Pentecost with a festival of its "rebirth." Others set the festival on the Sunday after the Nativity of St. John the Baptist (June 24), since the Augsburg Confession was promulgated on June 25, 1530. These early observances died out quickly.

The outbreak of the Thirty Years' War, which found the Roman princes engaged in a final attempt to wipe out north European Protestantism, created a renewed anti-Roman spirit

[12] Cf. Horn, op. cit., p. 76, where he quotes from Daniel on this point.
[13] Luther was born on November 10, 1483 (St. Martin's Eve), and his Christian name he owes to Martin of Tours.

typified in the Swedish Lutheran "Lion of the North," Gustavus
Adolphus, who, though he lost his life in the Battle of Lützen
(1632) saved the Protestant cause. In 1667, John George II,
Elector of Saxony, ordered a Festival of the Reformation to be
celebrated on October 31. The festival spread, and following
the seventeenth- and eighteenth-century trend of moving weekday festivals to the nearest Sunday, the Sunday either immediately before or after October 31 came to be observed as
Reformation Sunday. In recent years the day has been taken
up in nonliturgical circles through its promotion by the National Council of Churches of Christ in the United States of
America.

One disastrous effect, so far as the Lutheran church is concerned, is that All Saints' Day (November 1), an ancient and
important festival of the ecumenical church, has been overshadowed by a newer and more sectarian occasion. If, as is
likely, the Festival of the Reformation must be retained in
Lutheran calendars and is to be celebrated on a Sunday, its
observance should be restricted to the Sunday before October
31, with All Saints' Day allowed an equal observance on the
Sunday after November 1. It is interesting to note that Muhlenberg, while he follows the church year quite carefully both in
public services and in his private meditation and devotion, does
not include or refer to this festival.

Propers: Introit—Ps. 46:7, 2, 1
　　　　　Collect—Church Order of Duke Henry
　　　　　　of Saxony, 1539
　　　　　Lesson—1 Sam. 3:19—4:1a
　　　　　Epistle—Rom. 3:21-28
　　　　　Gradual—Ps. 48:1, 12, 13, 14
　　　　　Gospel—John 8:31-36
　　　　　Creed—Nicene

Proper Preface—All Saints
Color—Red

ALL SAINTS' DAY — NOVEMBER 1

As early as the third century, the primitive church provided a celebration for all martyrs. In the next century we know that the date of the festival was May 13, and this date was adopted in the West when the old Roman Pantheon was rebuilt and dedicated to St. Mary and All Martyrs on May 13, 610. The Pantheon had been built by Agrippa in 27 B.C., but by the seventh century, the cost of maintaining the old building had become burdensome to the government and the Emperor Phocas gave it to Pope Boniface IV.

A century later Pope Gregory III (731-741) dedicated a chapel in St. Peter's to "all the apostles, martyrs, confessors and all the just and perfect who are at rest." The date of the commemoration remained on May 13 until 835 when Pope Gregory IV (827-844) shifted it to November 1. One reason for the change is believed to have been the popularity of the festival, which attracted large numbers of pilgrims. The food supply in Rome in May was insufficient to care for them.

In northern Europe the day was one of holy obligation in the Middle Ages and was extremely popular in England, France, Ireland and Germany. In France, it was one of the four weekday festivals which survived in the Concordat of Napoleon (along with Christmas, the Ascension and the Assumption).

All Saints' Day is a holy day of obligation for American Roman Catholics.[14] In the Roman Catholic church the day has

---

[14] Holy days of obligation in the Roman Catholic church in the United States are: all the Sundays of the year; the Circumcision; the Ascension; the Assumption; All Saints' Day; the Immaculate Conception; Christmas. The dates, except for the Ascension, are: January 1, August 15, November 1, December 8, respectively.

had an octave since the time of Pope Sixtus IV (1471-1484). In the Anglican and many Lutheran calendars, All Saints' Day was ranked as a minor, rather than a major, festival. The *Service Book* restores it to major status. In some Lutheran churches, All Saints' Day, or the Sunday following, is the occasion for a parochial service in commemoration of the faith·ful departed. In medieval times there was often a perambulation of the churchyard cemetery on either All Saints' Day or All Souls' Day (November 2). Certainly it is a more fitting occasion for a *Todtenfest* than either St. Sylvester's Day (December 31) or the Last Sunday after Trinity.

> *Propers:* Introit—Rev. 7:14, 15a; Ps. 33:1
> Collect—*Book of Common Prayer,* 1549
> Lesson—Deut. 33:1-3
> Epistle—Rev. 7:2-17
> Gradual—Ps. 34:9, 10b; Matt. 11:28
> Gospel—Matt. 5:1-12
> Creed—Nicene
> Proper Preface—All Saints
> Color—Red

A DAY OF GENERAL OR SPECIAL THANKSGIVING

In American Lutheran use, the propers for this day are used on Thanksgiving Day, the fourth Thursday in November, though the *Service Book* also provides propers for the Festival of Harvest which are appropriate too. The first American Thanksgiving Day was observed by the Plymouth Pilgrims in 1621, and was followed sporadically by proclamations issued by colonial governors from time to time. The Continental Congress made Thanksgiving Day a national observance during the Revolution, but after the war national thanksgiving days were proclaimed only after special events, such as the adoption of the Constitution, peace after the War of 1812, etc. It was not until the Civil War that Abraham Lincoln inaugurated the custom of an annual national thanksgiving day. The date was the last Thursday in November to the time of President Franklin D. Roosevelt, when the date was set as the fourth Thursday in November.

The proper service for a Day of Thanksgiving is Matins, which includes the canticle, *Te Deum laudamus,* but propers for the service on such an occasion are not unknown in the sixteenth-century Lutheran church orders.

> *Propers:* Introit—Ps. 150:6, 2, 1
> Collect—*Church Book,* 1878
> Lesson—Deut. 8:1-20 or Isa. 61:10-11
> Epistle—1 Tim. 2:1-8 or Acts 14:8-18
> Gradual—Pss. 145:15-16; 103:1, 2
> Gospel—Matt. 6:25-33
> Creed—Nicene or Apostles'
> Proper Preface—none
> Color—Red

THE FESTIVAL OF HARVEST

The custom of thanksgiving after harvest is probably as old as religion. Among the ancient Hebrews, Pentecost was originally a harvest festival before it received its later significance as the anniversary of the delivery of the Law to Moses on Mt. Sinai. The Feast of the Booths (or Tabernacles; or Succoth) which took place in Tisri (September) was a thanksgiving for the harvest of grapes and olives, as Pentecost had been for grain. The fall Ember Days (after September 14), probably replaced a Roman harvest festival. The Swiss Reformed church has a *Herbstcommunion* in September which occurs about the time of Succoth.[15]

---

[15] Alt, *op. cit.,* p. 535, connects it with Succoth.

In England, August 1 (St. Peter's Chains) was Lammas (Loaf Mass) and a thanksgiving for the wheat harvest. Many Lutheran church orders provided for harvest festival services, though there was no agreement on dates. Some orders observed it on Michaelmas (September 29) and others ordered it on either the Sunday preceding or following Michaelmas. The current calendar of the Evangelishe Kirche in Deutschland, reflecting present German custom, prescribes it for the First Sunday after Michaelmas, except when this Sunday falls in September, in which case the *Erntedankfest* is observed on the first Sunday in October. In rural America, even in nonliturgical churches, such a festival is often observed under the name of Harvest Home.

In America, the propers for the Festival of Harvest are sometimes used on Thanksgiving Day.

> *Propers:* Introit—Ps. 65:11, 9a, 10b, 1
> Collect—*Church Book,* 1868
> Lesson—Deut. 11:8-21
> Epistle—Acts 14:11-18
> Gradual—Pss. 145:15, 16; 103:1, 2
> Gospel—Luke 12:15-34
> Creed—Nicene or Apostles'
> Proper Preface—none
> Color—Red

A DAY OF HUMILIATION AND PRAYER

Some Lutheran orders retained the historic Rogation Days (*q.v.*) and the quarterly Ember Days (*q.v.*) but others substituted periodic days of penance. Sometimes these were on specified dates; more often they were on proclamation by either the church or the temporal ruler. In some cases, such days were as frequent as once a month; in others, once a quarter. Among the early orders specifying days of humiliation and prayer are the Reformation of Hesse (1526), Lüneberg (1527), Mecklenburg (1552), Cassel (1539) and Württemberg (1568). The days could hardly have said to be popular, and, in modern America, the propers are seldom used.

Propers: Introit—Isa. 1:2, 4b; 130:3
     Collect—Nuremberg Church Order, 1691
     Lesson—1 Sam. 7:3-12
     Epistle—Acts 3:12-19a
     Gradual—Isa. 55:6, 7
     Gospel—Matt. 7:6-12
     Creed—Nicene or Apostles'
     Proper Preface—none
     Color—Black

OTHER DAYS OBSERVED IN SOME
LUTHERAN CALENDARS

In addition to the days in the calendar of the *Service Book* of the Lutheran church in America, there are other days which are in Lutheran calendars and deserve mention. The observance of holy days has never had in the Lutheran church the degree of agreement which has existed in both the Roman Catholic church and the Anglican church.

At the time of the Reformation, the calendar was still to some degree in the hands of the bishops or of regional synods. The calendars of Mainz, Cologne and Bamberg, for instance, like those of Salisbury (Sarum) and York in England, agreed with one another in the main, but differed in minor but sometimes important details. In the sixteenth century, uniformity did not appear as important as did the right of each diocese to regulate importance of existing days, or even to create new ones.

Nor did the political situation in Lutheran lands favor uniformity. Germany did not exist at all as a nation, but only as a congeries of more or less independent duchies, electorates, city-states and kingdoms, some with complete, and others with some degree of, autonomy which was jealously guarded against encroachments by either its neighbors or by some centralized authority. This was far different from the situation in England where the king headed the Anglican church. In Lutheran areas, however, no single church order was possible. Each political area adopted its own church order, including its calendar. This gave rise to a wide variety of customs and ceremonies. It also resulted in a wide variety of holy days. Some of these, like Corpus Christi, soon disappeared entirely from Lutheran calendars; others, like St. Mary Magdalene, continue in many Lutheran calendars.

In addition there was not then nor has there been since any central authority in the Lutheran church comparable to the Roman Curia which has the power to make changes in the calendar, or to secure uniformity of observance; nor is there anything comparable to the *Ordo Romanum* which prescribes liturgical observances year by year and diocese by diocese. It is doubtful if there ever will be or should be, since Lutherans have always viewed such matters as adiaphora. In theory, it would be perfectly proper for a Lutheran congregation to commemorate St. Ambrose of Milan if it chose to do so, or to omit the Feast of SS. Simon and Jude as many do. The only force leading towards uniformity in the calendar is that of general acceptance, taste, tradition, and common sense.

In view of all this, it is not surprising that Lutheran calendars have exhibited, and still exhibit, a wide variety. *All* of the sixteenth-century church orders include the following days: all Sundays of the year; Christmas (from one to three days); The Circumcision, although it is sometimes called New Year's Day;

the Epiphany; the Presentation or Candlemas (in German, *Maria Lichtmesse*); the Annunciation; Easter (from one to three days); the Ascension; Pentecost (from one to three days); the Nativity of St. John the Baptist.

More than half of the sixteenth-century church orders include, in addition to the above, the following: SS. John, Peter and Paul, Michael, Andrew, Thomas, Matthias, Philip, James, Bartholomew, Simon, Jude, Matthew, Mark, Luke, Mary Magdalene, Lawrence; the Visitation, Maundy Thursday, Good Friday, All Saints. Over a third include: SS. Stephen, Nicholas, Anne, Martin, Ansgar, Lucy, Barnabas; the Conversion of St. Paul, Trinity Sunday, the Assumption, the Nativity of the Virgin Mary, the Decollation of St. John the Baptist, St. Peter's Chains, Holy Innocents, Corpus Christi, the Invention of the Cross, the Exaltation of the Cross, All Souls', Ash Wednesday.

But the following days were retained in one or more of the sixteenth-century orders: SS. Catherine, Barbara, Thomas of Canterbury, Sylvester, Henriks, Erik, Eskil, Botolf, Olaf, Bernard of Clairvaux, Augustine, Francis of Assisi, Birgitta, Cecilia, Elizabeth, Blasius, Gregory the Great, Ambrose of Milan, George; the Major Litany; the 10,000 Widows; the 11,000 Virgins; the Holy Angels; St. Peter's Chair, and Reformation Day.

In addition, many orders retained the Ember Days, though they changed the emphasis; and the Rogation Days.

THE EMBER DAYS

The Ember Days which originated in Rome possibly as early as the third century (Pope Callixtus I, 218-225) were the Wednesday, Friday and Saturday following Pentecost, the Exaltation of the Holy Cross (September 14), and St. Lucy (December 13). Later there was added the Wednesday, Friday and Saturday after the First Sunday in Lent. The three

earlier Ember Days correspond to ancient pagan Roman celebrations connected with the harvest (Pentecost), the vintage
(September), and sowing (December). The three original
embertides were undoubtedly Christian fasts connected with
agriculture and the fruits of the earth and had some of the
same characteristics as the Rogation Days. Under Pope
Gelasius I (492-496) however, this early agrarian character
was replaced by an association of the four seasons with the
ordination of the clergy, an association retained in the Roman
Catholic church to the present, though the days are still pri-
marily days of fasting, penitence and prayer.

From their Roman beginnings, the Ember Days spread
slowly in Europe. In England, they were adopted by the
Council of Cloveshoe in 747. They were introduced into
Germany by St. Boniface. Charlemagne adopted them for his
empire in 769. They were adopted in Spain in the eleventh
century, and were introduced into the Ambrosian calendar at
Milan by St. Charles Barromeo in the sixteenth century. The
dates of the Ember Days were finally established by Pope
Gregory VII (1073-1085).

The name "ember" is a corruption of the German word
quatember which is in turn a corruption of the Latin *quattuor
tempore*. Though the Ember Days were taken over by the
Anglicans in their calendar, they became in the Lutheran
church days of quarterly lectures and examinations in the
catechism, though they continued to be listed in some Lutheran
calendars. The Wittenberg church order of 1533 specified two
sessions of catechetical instruction on the Monday, Tuesday,
Thursday and Friday of the first two weeks in Lent and Advent,
Holy Cross week and the week following, and the two weeks
after the Harvest Festival.[16] It was not long, however, before

[16] Alt, *op. cit.*, p. 442; Lindberg, *op. cit.*, p. 385-6. It is probable that the
Holy Cross week was in May, the week of the Invention of the Holy Cross
(May 3), rather than after the Exaltation of the Holy Cross (September 14).

the catechetical lectures fell into disuse and were replaced by other more thorough methods of instruction. With their disappearance, the Ember Days disappeared from most Lutheran calendars. This is unfortunate from an ecumenical and liturgical point of view, particularly since there was nothing in them that was in the least doctrinally objectionable.

THE ROGATION DAYS

The Rogation Days are three days, Monday, Tuesday, and Wednesday, before Ascension Day and following Rogate, the Fifth Sunday after Easter. They are characterized by processions (*Bittgänge*, in German) and the recitation of litanies. Though there had been such litanies and processions before his time,[17] they had been sporadic, and it was Bishop Mamertus of Vienne (France) who instituted the Rogation Days about 470. The immediate cause is thought to have been either an earthquake, pestilence, or barbarian invasions. The First Council of Orleans in 511 made these days binding on all Gallican churches. The Council of Cloveshoe adopted them for England in 747. At Rome they were adopted during the pontificate of Leo III (795-816). As time passed, the nature of the ceremonies changed from one of petition against invasion and untoward "acts of God" to one of solemn prayer for a fruitful harvest and the blessing of the fields. The tone remained, however, penitential, and the color worn was violet with both the *Gloria in excelsis* and the creed being omitted from the services. The procession started from a church, proceeded around the parish boundaries while psalms and litanies were said, and ended in another church where the mass concluded the ceremonies of the day.

In the Middle Ages in England the days were known as

---

[17] The custom is of Eastern origin and goes back at least to the time of the fourth-century Arian controversy.

Gange Days (in Germany, *Bittgänge*) and the procession was called "beating the bounds of the parish." In time it became a somewhat riotous occasion with banners, handbells, ale, wine and sometimes a barbecue. It was also known as "rogationing" or "perambulating." This was a far cry from the processional litanies described by Gregory of Tours in which the people, often barefoot and clad in black, walked in solemn procession behind a crucifer and sometimes carried the book of gospels and relics of the patron saint. The English processions were sobered somewhat by Queen Elizabeth. In some English parishes they continue to the present.

In recent years, in nonliturgical American churches, Rogate Sunday has become Rural Life Sunday. By an exchange of pulpits between rural and urban ministers, it is hoped that more mutual understanding will be created. In some Lutheran churches there has been a revival of special services of prayer and intercession for a fruitful season, and some revival of the office of the blessing of the fields. Unfortunately, these efforts usually have been set on Rogate Sunday which is a festival and not a penitential day.

The Rogation Days were retained by some Lutheran church orders of the sixteenth century on the traditional days of the Monday, Tuesday and Wednesday before the Ascension. More often, however, the Rogation Days were replaced by penitential days set by proclamation.[18] Wittingly or not, this was a return to the situation as it was before Mamertus of Vienne in the fifth century.

ST. BARNABAS — JUNE 11

St. Barnabas has really more claim to apostolic rank than many of the members of the original band of the disciples. And much more is known of him and his labors for the faith than

[18] Cf. A Day of Humiliation and Prayer, *supra*.

is known of most of the twelve. He was one of the leaders of the apostolic church. It was he who sought out Saul and brought him to Antioch (Acts 11:22-26). He and St. Paul were set apart as the first missionaries to the Gentiles (Acts 13:2-3) and set out together on the first extended missionary journey. Early church tradition included Barnabas as one of the seventy (Luke 10:1). His name, along with that of St. Stephen is included in the Roman canon of the mass. He appears to have been considered an apostle by the primitive church (1 Cor. 9:1-6) and his name is often included in the medieval lists of the apostles. Some Lutheran orders retained his day specifically; others implied it when they stated simply "all apostles' days."

A fifth century tradition says that Barnabas met his death at Salamis in Cyprus, being stoned to death at the hands of the Jews there. In the East his festival dates from the fifth century. In the West it occurs first in a ninth century calendar of Naples; it became accepted at Rome in the eleventh century.

Although St. Barnabas never succeeded in having a strong European *cultus,* his day was retained in the Anglican calendar. On every ground, St. Barnabas is worthy of a place in even the most conservative calendar.

ST. MARY MAGDALENE, PENITENT — JULY 22

A day very popular in pre-Reformation Germany and the retention of which was favored by Luther himself, was the festival of St. Mary Magdalene, Penitent. Many sixteenth-century calendars retained the day and the present calendar of the Lutheran Church—Missouri Synod retains it.

Mary Magdalene is identified as the sister of Lazarus and Martha of Bethany, and usually as the woman possessed by seven devils (Mark 16:9; Luke 8:2). In St. John's Gospel, she is the first to greet our Lord on Easter morning in the

Garden. There is a wealth of tradition about her post-resurrection activities. One tradition places her death and burial at Ephesus. Another tradition takes her to southern Gaul and her reputed relics are said to be in the Monastery of Vezelay, near Autun, France. Her day, the same date both East and West is July 22, and appears in church calendars from the tenth century. It was a very popular festival in northern Europe, and was a holy day of obligation in France and in the archdiocese of Cologne.

ST. LAWRENCE, MARTYR — AUGUST 10

St. Lawrence, a deacon of the church at Rome, was martyred on a gridiron in the third century. A man of great piety, his martyrdom is one of the earliest in the Western church, and his day one of the oldest in the Western calendar. The details of his life and death are well attested.

For many centuries, St. Lawrence's Day occupied a place of importance equal to SS. Peter and Paul (June 29) and St. Michael (September 29) as being one of the days which subdivided the time after Pentecost into smaller cycles. The period from Pentecost to SS. Peter and Paul represented the apostolic age; from SS. Peter and Paul to St. Lawrence, the age of persecution of the primitive church; from St. Lawrence to St. Michael, the church at work in the world at present; and from St. Michael to Advent, the expectant church looking forward to the Second Advent.

The day was of great importance in the Western church and was provided with a vigil and an octave, a ranking equal to the Circumcision and Trinity Sunday and above most of the apostles' days. In the Middle Ages it was a holy day of obligation at Cologne, Treves, and elsewhere, losing that dignity only as the hierarchy tended more and more to make the Assumption (which occurs only five days later, on August 15) a holy day of obligation. Many Lutheran churches in Germany are named in honor of St. Lawrence, and his day was retained in a number of sixteenth-century church orders.

The annual meteoric showers that recur each August (Perseids) are known popularly as "the tears of St. Lawrence."

———————

The entire matter of the calendar needs serious study, especially in regard to saints' days and other festivals. If it is true that the pre-Reformation plethora of holy days surfeited the people, it is also true that the ultra-conservatism of both the extreme Lutheran and Anglican reformers (which is the tradition which has come down to us at least as far as the calendar is concerned) has robbed the church of much of the sense of the continuity of the church as expressed in the lives of godly men and women of every age. We can be reminded of them without seeking their intercession. We can admire their faith without attempting to appropriate their good works. And we need to be reminded of that "great cloud of witnesses" cheering us along our Christian way.

BIBLIOGRAPHY

BIBLIOGRAPHY

THE CALENDAR

Alt, Heinrich. *Das Kirchenjahr.* Berlin, 1860.

Cabrol, Fernand. *Holy Week.* New York: P. J. Kenedy & Sons, 1926.

————. *The Year's Liturgy.* 2 volumes. Vol. I: Seasons. New York: Benziger Bros., 1939. Vol. II: The Sanctoral. London: Burns, Oates & Washbourne, 1940.

Daniel, H. A. *Codex liturgicus ecclesiae universae.* 4 volumes. Leipzig, 1847.

Dowden, John. *The Church Year and Calendar.* Cambridge: The University Press, 1910.

Horn, Edward T. *The Christian Year.* Philadelphia: Lutheran Book Store, 1876.

Kellner, K. A. Heinrich. *Heortology.* English translation of the 2nd German ed. London: Kegan Paul, Trench, Trübner & Co., 1908.

Lindberg, Gustaf. *Kyrkans Heliga Ar.* Stockholm: Svenska Kyrkans Diakonistyrelses Bokförlag, 1937.

McArthur, A. Alan. *The Evolution of the Christian Year.* London: S.P.C.K., 1953.

Parsch, Pius. *The Church's Year of Grace.* 4 volumes. Collegeville, Minn., 1953.

Schmid, Franz X. *Liturgik der christkathol. Religion.* 3 volumes. Vol. 3, pp. 441-610, treats of the festivals. Passau, 1831.

Sehling, Emil (ed.). *Die evangelischen Kirchenordnungen des XVI Jahrhunderts.* 5 volumes. Leipzig, 1902-13.

Staley, Vernon. *The Liturgical Year.* London: A. R. Mowbray & Co., 1907.

————. *The Seasons, Fasts and Festivals of the Christian Year.* London: A. R. Mowbray & Co., 1910.

Stedman, Joseph F. *My Lenten Missal.* Brooklyn: The Confraternity of the Precious Blood, 1941.

Strauss, Friedrich. *Das evangelische Kirchenjahr in seinem Zusammenhange dargestelt.* Berlin, 1850.

Strodach, Paul Zellner. *The Church Year.* Philadelphia: The United Lutheran Publication House, 1924.

———. *The Collect for the Day.* Philadelphia: The United Lutheran Publication House, 1939.

SERVICE BOOKS AND COMMENTARIES

Baillet, Adrian. *Les Vies des Saints.* 2nd ed. Paris, 1703. Vol. IX on history of movable feasts.

Bäumer, Suitbert. *Geschichte des Breviers.* Freiburg, 1895.

Campion. W. M., and Beamont, W. J. *The Prayer Book Interleaved.* London: Rivington, 1866.

Clarke, W. K. Lowther, and Harris, Charles (eds.). *Liturgy and Worship.* London: S.P.C.K., 1947.

Duchesne, L. *Christian Worship.* 5th English ed., translated by M. L. McClure. London: S.P.C.K., 1949.

Feltoe, Charles L. (ed.). *Sacramentarium Leonianum.* Cambridge, 1896.

Fortescue, Adrian. *The Mass.* London: Longmans, Green & Co., 1917.

———. *The Ceremonies of the Roman Rite Described.* London: Burns, Oates & Washbourne, 1943.

Gebert, Martin. *Vetus Liturgia Alemannica.* Part III, Disquisitio IX, De Festis. Typis San-Blasianis, 1776.

Hoeynck, F. A. *Geschichte der kirchlich Liturgie des Distums Augsburg.* Augsburg, 1889.

Lotz, Walter (ed.). *Geistliche Waffenrüstung.* Kassel: Johannes Stauda, 1947.

Maskell, William. *Monumenta Ritualia Ecclesiae Anglicanae.* 3 volumes. London: William Pickering, 1846.

Proctor, Francis, and Frere, Walter Howard. *A New History of the Book of Common Prayer.* London: Macmillan & Co., 1907.

Reed, Luther D. *The Lutheran Liturgy.* Philadelphia: The Muhlenberg Press, 1947.

Shepherd, Massey Hamilton, Jr. *The Oxford American Prayer Book Commentary.* New York: Oxford University Press, 1950.

———. *The Worship of the Church.* Greenwich, Conn.: The Seabury Press, 1952.

Staley, Vernon. *The Ceremonial of the English Church.* 4th ed., rev. London: A. R. Mowbray & Co., 1927.

Wilson, H. A. (ed.). *The Gelasian Sacramentary.* Oxford, 1894.

———. *The Gregorian Sacramentary.* Vol. XLIX, Henry Bradshaw Society. London, 1915.

Missale Romanum. Editio VI Post Alteram Typicam. Ratisbon, Rome, New York & Cincinnati, 1906.

The Missal (in English). London: Burns & Oates, 1920. Edited by Adrian Fortescue.

Ordo (Officii Recitandi et Missae Celebrandae juxta Kalendar, etc.) New York & Cincinnati, 1944.

A Short Breviary. Edited by the Monks of St. John's Abbey. Collegeville, Minn.: St. John's Abbey Press, 1941.

And the writings of the following in Migne's *Latin Fathers:* Isidore of Seville (Vol. LXXXIII); Amalarius (CV); Rabanus Maurus (CVII); Ado (CXXIII); Berno of Reichenau (CXLII); Hugo of St. Victor (CLXXVII); Rupert of Deutz (CLXX); Honorius of Autun (CLXXII); Sicardus (CCXIII); Innocent III (CCXVII).

The Bamberg (1499), Constance (1505) and Nürnberg (1484) Missals and the Augsburg Breviary (1535) in the Krauth Memorial Library, Philadelphia.

GENERAL

Brilioth, Yngve. *Eucharistic Faith and Practice.* London, 1930.

Cabrol, Fernand. *The Mass of the Western Rites.* New York, 1934.

Horn, Edward T. *Outlines of Liturgics.* Philadelphia, 1890.

King, Archdale A. *Liturgies of the Religious Orders.* London, 1955.

Maxwell, W. D. *An Outline of Christian Worship.* Oxford. 1936.

Srawley, J. H. *The Early History of the Liturgy.* 2nd ed. Cambridge, 1947.

West, R. C. *Western Liturgies.* London, 1938.

Will, Robert. *Le Culte.* 3 volumes. Strasburg and Paris, 1925-1935.

INDEX

INDEX

Absolution, 121
Acolyte, 43
Adoration of the Cross, 125
Advent, 9, 10, 24, 25, 39, 54-65, 77, 135ff, 150, 191, 198, 220
   Color, 48-51
   Images, 59
   Sunday (*See* First Sunday in Advent)
   Sunday Next Before, 86, 174
   First Sunday in, 56, 60-61, 88, 117, 135, 150
   Second Sunday in, 61-62
   Third Sunday in, 63-64 (*See also* Gaudete)
   Fourth Sunday in, 59, 64-65
Aeon, 17, 82
Agrippa, 209
Alcuin, 158
Alexander II, 158
Alexandria, 15, 17, 67, 82, 134, 192, 195
Alleluia, 28, 34, 45-46, 55, 95-96, 99, 102, 132, 138, 161ff, 165
Alleluia, dulce carmen, 96
All Hallows' Eve, 189, 206ff (*See also* Reformation Day)
All Saints' Day, 42, 147, 176, 181, 206ff, 209ff, 215
   Color, 48-49, 52
All Souls' Day, 176, 210, 215
Altar, 48
Altar Guild, 48
Altar of Repose, 122, 125
Altar hangings, 48
Ambo, 43-44
Ambrosian rite, 31, 41, 148, 216 (*See also* Milan)

Amen, 28, 34
Amenemhet I, 82
Amiens, 196
Anabaptists, 122
Anglicans, 1, 5, 6, 24, *passim*
Anjou, Duke of, 202
Anniversary of a church, 52
Annunciation, 24, 49, 52, 68, 77, 78, 105, 136, 178, 190ff, 198, 215 (*See also* **Virgin Mary**)
Antecommunion, 6
Antioch, 22, 67, 147, 204, 219
Antiphon, 37-39, 56-57, 148
Antiphonary, 29
Antitrinitarians, 122
Apocrypha, 156, 159, 171
Apostles' days, 48, 52 (*See* individual saints)
Apostolic Tradition, 100, 124
Appearing of Christ, Feast of (*See* Epiphany)
Appian Way, 197
Arabia, 201
Arianism, 67
Armenia, 188, 202, 206
Armistice Day, 26
Ascension Day, 9, 21, 22, 128, 135ff, 146ff, 209, 215, 217
Ascensiontide, 50, 146ff
Ash Wednesday, 43, 49, 51, 52, 96, 102, 104, 105-107, 115, 121, 127, 135ff, 215
Ashes, Blessing of, 105-106
Asia Minor, 82
Ass, Feast of, 85 (*See* Epiphany, Octave of)
Augsburg Confession, 7, 207
Augustinians, 206

Type used in this book
Body, 12 on 14 Garamond
Display, Tempo Heavy

Paper: "GM" White Standard Antique